CARNIVAL CHINA

China in the Era of
Hu Jintao and Xi Jinping

CARNIVAL CHINA

China in the Era of
Hu Jintao and Xi Jinping

Kerry Brown

University of Sydney, Australia

Imperial College Press

Published by

Imperial College Press
57 Shelton Street
Covent Garden
London WC2H 9HE

Distributed by

World Scientific Publishing Co. Pte. Ltd.
5 Toh Tuck Link, Singapore 596224
USA office: 27 Warren Street, Suite 401-402, Hackensack, NJ 07601
UK office: 57 Shelton Street, Covent Garden, London WC2H 9HE

British Library Cataloguing-in-Publication Data
A catalogue record for this book is available from the British Library.

CARNIVAL CHINA
China in the Era of Hu Jintao and Xi Jinping

ISBN 978-1-78326-424-7

Typeset by Stallion Press
Email: enquiriesstallionpress.com

Dedicated to David Hayes of Open Democracy, in recognition of his immense help in publishing and supporting these essays, and to Georgia Regan, for her immense help in editing and arranging them.

Author Bio

Kerry Brown is Executive Director of the China Studies Centre, and Professor of Chinese Politics at the University of Sydney. He leads the Europe China Research and Advice Network (ECRAN), funded by the European Commission, and is an Associate Fellow on the Asia Programme at Chatham House. Prior to this he was Head of the Asia Programme at Chatham House. Educated at Cambridge, London and Leeds Universities, he worked in Japan and the Inner Mongolian region of China, before joining the Foreign and Commonwealth Office in London. He worked in the China Section and then served as First Secretary, Beijing, from 2000 to 2003, and Head of the Indonesia East Timor Section at the Foreign & Commonwealth Office (FCO) from 2003 to 2005.

He is the author of *The Cultural Revolution in Inner Mongolia* (Global Oriental Ltd, 2006), *Struggling Giant: China in the 21st Century* (Anthem Press, 2007), *The Rise of the Dragon — Chinese Investment Flows in the Reform Period* (Chandos Publishing, 2008), *Friends and Enemies: The Past, Present and Future of the Communist Party of China* (Anthem Press, 2009), *Ballot Box China* (Zed Books Ltd, 2011), *China 2020* (editor, Chandos Press, 2012), *Hu Jintao, China's Silent Leader* (World Scientific, 2012), *Contemporary China* (Palgrave MacMillan, 2013), and *The Networked Leadership: China's Fifth Generation Leaders* (IBTauris, 2014). *The EU and China: A Policy Manual in Politics and Economics*, will be published by Imperial College Press in 2014, as well as a collection of longer papers he has edited with Palgrave Macmillan. He is the chief editor of the *Berkshire Dictionary of Chinese Biography* to be published in early 2014.

John Keane is Professor of Politics at the University of Sydney.

Foreword

The booming business of China-watching and China assessment has produced an assortment of glib orthodoxies, none more potent than the conclusion that the political system of China is "authoritarian". The grip of phrases such as "authoritarianism", "authoritarian rule" and "authoritarian capitalism" arguably stems from their imprecision, hence from their malleability in the hands of a wide range of scholars, journalists, politicians and pundits, all of whom like to portray China as an "authoritarian regime", often to suit their own scholarly and political standpoints.

Consider some well-known examples. The American businessman James McGregor speaks of China as a "one-of-a-kind system of authoritarian capitalism that is in danger of terminating itself — and taking the world down with it". The Chinese political experiment, he says, resembles a hybrid combination of the so-called Gilded Age and the Robber Baron era.[1] Surprisingly similar language is used, for quite different purposes, by the darling of the hard Left, the Bolshevik Slavoj Žižek, who insists that the virus of "authoritarian capitalism is slowly but surely spreading around the globe, nowhere more so than China". Žižek questions the claim that "political democracy" is "the 'natural' political accompaniment of capitalism" by posing a provocative question: "What if China's authoritarian capitalism is not a stop on the road to further democratization, but the end state toward which the rest of the world is headed?"[2] With less flourish, more than a few Atlantic-region political scientists sing the same refrain. They describe China either as a straightforward case of an "authoritarian regime",

---

[1] James McGregor, *No Ancient Wisdom, No Followers: the Challenges of Chinese Authoritarian Capitalism*, Prospecta Press, Westport, CT, 2012, p. 60.
[2] Slavoj Žižek, "Capitalism: How the Left Lost the Argument", *Foreign Policy*, November 2012.

or as a strange new form of "fragmented authoritarianism", a polity whose rulers "show signs of responsiveness" to the "increasingly diverse demands of Chinese society", but nonetheless a political system that remains "authoritarian" to its one-party state foundations.[3]

What these contrasting interpretations of China have in common is their deep attachment both to the nebulous notion of authoritarianism and the belief that an "authoritarian regime" is the opposite of "democracy". Some observers tap this presumption for the purpose of welcoming the historic trend towards "post-democracy".[4] Others mobilise the same conviction to warn of the "rise of China", or of the "China menace". Great power theorists are especially concerned with the way rising powers provoke war with established hegemons, such as the United States. They say that the ascent of "authoritarian" China is the defining story of our age; or that its system of "market authoritarianism" confronts the global order with the great new challenge of rekindling "the drive among others to acquire and preserve democratic freedoms".[5]

The claim that "authoritarian" China is fundamentally at odds with American-style "democracy" has a notable pedigree (traceable to a classic essay on the subject by Samuel Huntington[6]), but it is an unpersuasive platitude. Such is the contention made in *Carnival China* by distinguished China specialist and public intellectual Kerry Brown, and this wonderful study of contemporary China is no ordinary book. Indeed, it is remarkable in several ways.

[3] Andrew Mertha, "'Fragmented Authoritarianism 2.0': Political Pluralization in the Chinese Policy Process", *The China Quarterly*, December 2009, pp. 995–1012.

[4] Eric Xi Li, "The Life of the Party: The Post-Democratic Future Begins in China", *Foreign Affairs*, January/February 2013.

[5] Stefan Halper, *The Beijing Consensus: How China's Authoritarian Model Will Dominate the Twenty-First Century*, Basic Books, New York, 2010, p. xii; Other examples include Robert D. Kaplan, "How We Would Fight China", *Atlantic Monthly*, June 2005; Ross Terrill, *The New Chinese Empire*, Basic Books, New York, 2003; Martin Jacques, *When China Rules the World*, Penguin, London, 2009.

[6] Samuel P. Huntington, *Authoritarian Politics in Modern Society*, Basic Books, New York, 1970; Pei Minxin, "A Discussion on Authoritarianism with Samuel Huntington, the Pioneer of the Theory of Authoritarianism", *Chinese Sociology & Anthropology*, Volume 23, 4, Summer 1991, pp. 67–75.

Most obviously, it is a ground-breaking interpretation of Chinese politics that openly admits its own biases, along the way strongly encouraging readers to nurture their own sense of wonder about the myriad dramatic and contradictory things that are going on in contemporary China. Brown shows that a common mistake among China analysts is their misplaced narcissism, their misjudged efforts to "find bones in an egg" (*jidan li tiao gu tou*), as the Chinese expression has it, as if China is best judged by their own political standards of "liberal democracy". In matters of China scholarship, he cautions against closed minds, along the way inviting readers to admit uncertainties, to explore their own ignorance, and above all to see that contemporary China is no simple or straightforward actuality, but instead a cauldron of contradictions, a kaleidoscope of confusing and conflicting trends, a "reality" which ought to make observers feel, in matters of observation, the truth of the common Chinese saying (*xiazi mo xiang*) that in these times all of us rather resemble the blind person sizing up different parts of an elephant that cannot be summarised in simple terms.

Fascinating and pleasurable to read in equal measure, this is a book that was never intended to be a book. Treated as a genre of writing, it's a fine set of field notes, let's say; a political anthropology of contemporary China that represents much more than an alluring chest of treasured observations of the bamboozling ins and outs of social and political trends in contemporary China. Brown shows that China is a state of mind, a way of using words. For him, words really count when analysing Chinese society and politics, just as they do elsewhere. He probes the prevailing language through which Chinese politics is analysed, and shows it to be wanting, badly. Not only does he cast doubt on the prejudice of those commentators and critics who suppose that "authoritarian" China is a standard post-communist polity tottering through a transition towards American-style "liberal democracy", itself the normative standard by which Chinese politics should be adjudged. Brown pushes much further. He shows in these pages that China cannot be described, loosely, lazily, unthinkingly, using the term "authoritarianism", to mean a type of regime in which established power supposes it has "authority", an absolute right to assert itself against its actual or potential opponents. Brown's objection is not that this way of describing things destroys the precious meaning and rich political significance of the root word "authority" (which it does). He instead demonstrates that when used as a synonym for haughty power whose agents suppose their own unquestionable superiority, the term "authoritarianism" wildly underestimates the carnivalesque lives of both the rulers and struggling citizens of China.

Chinese realities are bewildering. Contradictions are found in all leading institutions, at every street corner, in every nook and cranny of its vibrant multi-media scene. China is almost a fictional place, a country where tragedy and comedy come together on the same stage. China is a land where desperately poor and unhappy petitioners risk everything, even disappearance into terrifying black jails, for the sake of their dignity; a country where the strong prey on the weak, where a burgeoning middle class opposed to free multi-party elections is willing to stand up for more accountable and open government; a place where money making is called socialism; where there are more billionaires, skyscrapers and card-carrying communists than in the rest of the world.

On Brown's reckoning, China is most definitely not a "people's democracy", as its officials at all levels like to claim. It is certainly describable as a one-party-dominated political system marked by such well-recorded dysfunctions as vast undisclosed business fiefdoms, violence, censorship, corruption and hypocrisy. Parts of the system function in the totalitarian ways of old, using new methods, such as in the brutal repression of the Turkic-speaking citizens of Xinjiang. There are thuggish police tactics; excessive taxes designed to force land grabs; official brutality in crushing rebellions in the countryside. In the cities, there are the dreaded household registrations, enterprise layoffs, the confiscation of retirement pensions, arrests of those who want publicly to remind others that urban skies were once blue, or remember the Party's past crimes. China is also a land which simultaneously sings the praises of the winner of a Nobel Prize in Literature (Mo Yan) and cracks down hard on thousands of free-minded and honest writers; a country that silences rights lawyers and passes an Open Governance Law (in 2008); a polity run by governing officials who pride themselves by day on their commitments to the principles of open government, promotion by merit and "smart power" geared to serving "the people", all the while fostering forms of government by moonlight lubricated by binge drinking, delirious sex, conspicuous consumption and rivers of cash.

It is said that money makes the Chinese world go round, yet Brown points out that this is a labyrinthine political system, if system it can be called, in which political patronage and politics broadly defined is very much in command. Party officials know that money grows on the trees of political power. They know equally well the need to parade their political power. They dress and eat differently; as Brown points out, even their body smell is distinctive. They are naturally mindful of their vulnerability, which is why (for instance) vast sums of money are spent on domestic policing and surveillance, much more than on external military forces; and why, in order to rebuild damaged Party authority, since 1988, across more than 600,000 villages, there have been over a million elections, with some three million Party officials chosen by voters.[7] In the pages that follow, we are reminded that Party officials, like snakes after a long winter, have shed their belief in "socialism"; and we learn that a permanent tug-of-war between the authorities and those they try to rule is now a chronic feature of a political system that is sometimes so ramshackle, and so experimental, that it cannot accurately be described using any standard category drawn from political theory, or political science.

All things considered, what can be learned from reading this thoughtful, imaginative, illuminating book? Read on, reader, and you will surely discover, wherever you are, or whatever you believe, that China is not what it seems. Brown's fine study teaches us that to speak of China as an "authoritarian regime" is nonsense, simply because it ignores the "immensely complex and disunited" qualities of a quasi-imperial state that is both riddled with dysfunctions and yet "sort of unified, sort of in control of the main levers of the economy", and of the wider society. Brown's observations are especially astute on the subject of the Chinese Communist Party (CCP). Unlike the Communist Party of the Soviet Union, which collapsed like a house of cards in the winds of popular revolution during the period 1989–1991, the CCP has actively recruited members, many of them prominent and powerful figures in the fields of government, business, university and artistic life. The Party seeks to rule through wealth creation and "the appearance of

---

[7] Kerry Brown, *Ballot Box China: Grassroots Democracy in the Final Major One-Party State*, Zed Books Ltd, London, 2011.

consent". Its leadership treads carefully. It is acutely aware of the dangers of hubris and the need for government based on merit, performance and popular consent. Party leaders know well the Chinese proverb that powerful people fear fame just as pigs fear getting fat. They are well aware (says Brown) that the country grows "wealthier but scrappier, less harmonious and less content by the day". For this reason, China's dominant political class suffers from chronic anxiety. Its leadership, and plenty of its members, who make up only 7% of the whole population, seem at times to be almost neurotic, or perhaps proto-democratic, in their constant self-examination, self-justification and relentless attention-seeking. There are times (purchasing overseas property, for instance) when Party members act as if their time is fast running out. It comes as no surprise that they fear violent unrest, or that they are aware of the fine line that separates cowardice from civic courage. Hence their path-breaking laboratory experiments: their political interest in practices of open and publicly accountable government, such as live-streamed public forums, their calculated toleration of online public controversies and their hands-off attitudes to independently minded "public opinion leaders" (*yulun lingxiu*), figures such as the bad-boy blogger Han Han, the young model Gan Lulu and Yao Chen, the award-winning actress with a bold tongue and a huge Sina Weibo following.

Brown does not probe these latter trends in much detail, or ask whether there is any truth in the claim that China is "the advocate and builder of democracy"[8] with local characteristics, or whether perhaps the Chinese polity, slowly but surely, is becoming a strange simulacrum of the type of locally defined democratic vision sketched in documents such as the Charter 08 manifesto. Critics may say as well that Brown's account of the unfinished carnival of Chinese society and politics suffers from its excessive concentration on the "domestic"; that what's lost is the overriding fact that China, the fabled "workshop of the world", is now vigorously extending its planetary reach, from "soft power" diplomacy and mineral holdings in Africa, to currency markets in the West, to oilfields in the Middle East, to agribusiness in Latin America and Australia, to the factories of East Asia. The objection would be unfair, and not just because he has written about the

---

[8]Liu Jianfei, *Democracy and China*, New World Press, Beijing, 2011.

subject elsewhere, or that in these pages Brown argues forcefully against unthinking alarmism.[9] His smart and discerning study of the carnival called China spotlights the many ways China's global ambitions are held back by confusions and contradictions at home. Brown shows why China's rich and powerful rulers are finding it hard to win the world's love, why China's global presence is more broad than deep, and why, in other words, China is a "partial power"[10] that still lacks the domestic preconditions befitting a major world power.

More than anything else, Brown wisely teaches us to hold our breath. He knows that China will not escape the cast-iron rule that futures are never predictable. Using finely crafted words, he shows that the shape of things to come is always subject to the quantum principle of uncertainty, to the many not-yet-known causes and causers that shape people's lives, and their environments. This quantum principle trumps money, power and influence, and that's why Brown is right to say that when it comes to the future of China, its rich and greedy Party rulers and the whole wide world are in for some rude surprises.

John Keane
Sydney, November 2013

---

[9]See for example Kerry Brown, *Struggling Giant: China in the 21st Century*, Anthem Press, London, 2007; Kerry Brown (ed.), *China 2020: The Next Decade for the People's Republic of China*, Chandos Press, Oxford, 2011.

[10]David Shambaugh, *China Goes Global: The Partial Power*, Oxford University Press, New York, 2013.

Contents

Editorial Note and Acknowledgements

The essays are presented here much as they appeared first on the Open Democracy website, with some light editing. With the help of Georgia Regan, I have grouped them into thematic sections, supplying some introductory commentary. Within these sections, they follow a roughly chronological order. I have used Pinyin transliteration throughout. There are a few essays which have been jointly written. I am grateful for the co-authors of these pieces for working with me on these. I am immensely grateful to Isabel Hilton for originally introducing me to Open Democracy, and to David Hayes, who has been so instrumental in prompting me over the last few years to write pieces, and then editing them so diligently and thoroughly. I am also grateful for the editorial assistance of Georgia Regan on this book. I would also like to thank Jane Sayers, Tasha D'Cruz and the team at Imperial College Press for their assistance in publishing this book, and John Keane for furnishing it with a foreword. All errors and omissions remain my sole responsibility.

Introduction

"In fact, carnival does not know footlights, in the sense that it does not acknowledge any distinction between actors and spectators. . . . Carnival is not a spectacle seen by the people; they live in it, and everyone participates because its very idea embraces all the people. While carnival lasts, there is no other life outside it. During carnival time life is subject only to its laws, that is, the laws of its own freedom. It has a universal spirit; it is a special condition of the entire world, of the world's revival and renewal, in which all take part. Such is the essence of carnival, vividly felt by all its participants. . . . The tradition of the Saturnalias remained unbroken and alive in the medieval carnival, which expressed this universal renewal and was vividly felt as an escape from the usual official way of life."[1]

It seems strange to invoke the great literary theorist Mikhail Bakhtin at the start of a book about the People's Republic of China in the first decade of the 21st century. Bakhtin, after all, had written his first works during the dark years of the 1930s, even though he somehow survived into the 1970s, two decades after Stalin's death. Everything the People's Republic of China had become by the early 2000s was to get away from the shadow of the Soviet Union influence of the past, and the world that Bakhtin and people like him had come from. And yet, in his description of the anarchic world of Rabelais and the sorts of suspension of moral norms, normative statements and traditional codes of social behaviour understanding his work required, Bakhtin supplies an eerily fitting and appropriate framework to understand the contradictory, complex, dynamic and often baffling universe that China had become as it entered the sixth decade under Communist rule. Few words

---

[1] Mikhail Bakhtin (trans. Helene Iswolsky), *Rabelais and His World*, Indiana University Press, Bloomington, 1984, pp. 7, 8.

better captured this combination of drama, excitement, tragedy, confusion and sheer energy than "carnival".

Not that Chinese people themselves needed a dead Russian intellectual to guide them to this notion. In 2010, while having lunch with a good friend with whom I had previously worked as a diplomat in the early 2000s, he looked at me plaintively and simply said, "This place is like a fairy tale. Anything could happen. ANYTHING". The exhausted look of long-term residents as the decade wore on and we grew closer to the power transition expected by the elite political leadership in 2012 and 2013 was testimony to the fact that even those who thought after decades in China they had seen everything, began to sense that they had in fact not even seen the start! China had mutated for anyone who had lived there from the 1980s from a place that comfortably fitted the paradigm of a post-communist polity careering towards a messy transition where it would end up as something akin to the former Soviet Union (that was a common feeling in the early 1990s after the student uprising in June 1989 and its bloody repression) to somewhere utterly *sui generis*. A post-socialist state in economic behaviour, but one where the state was sort of unified, sort of in control of the main levers of the economy, but also immensely complex and disunited. A capitalist nation in the daily behaviour of its citizens but one still presided over by a Politburo Standing Committee, who lauded it over the dark terrain of politics while pretending they had nothing to do with the day-to-day running of the country. A place where social media and the internet were roasting officials alive for their venality, sexual sins and greed, but where the most vociferous users of these tools had a high chance of being shoved in jail for years if they strayed the wrong side of the ever-shifting invisible political red line. A country of billionaires and millions of desperate petitioners, of imprisoned artists and mistresses of the high and mighty in freefall, of a winner of a Nobel Prize in Literature able to walk around freely, and one of a Nobel Peace Prize laureate crammed in a jail for over a decade. China posed hard questions for itself and the world in being this way.

This bewilderment was as easy to be infected with as getting one of the foul, highly stubborn colds and throat infections that the polluted air in China's major cities often brought visitors and inhabitants as the decade wore on. I was struck with a particularly severe bout when engaged on what initially looked like a simple project in the summer of 2009 to try to understand foreign support for governance and public participation in decision making for a Europe-based think tank. My journey started in Beijing in early July, when storms finally broke over a city that had been in drought till then. The first people I interviewed simply told me that the situation for civil society actors and reformist-minded academics and officials had never been worse. The head of one major foreign non-governmental organisation (NGO) greeted me when I went to meet them with the simple statement, "You couldn't have come here at a worse time".

Society might have been growing visibly richer each day, but in the summer of 2009, only a year after the great Olympics when the city had been cleaned up, rebuilt, scrubbed and retrofitted so that in some parts it was unrecognisable, Beijing seemed to have a pall over it. One Chinese scholar, who has since tragically died, said that the rights lawyers who had so bravely represented some of the most contentious cases of the last few years — Falun Gong practitioners, Gao Zhisheng, the lawyer brutally tortured and beaten up, the then-detained but, as yet, not-charged Liu Xiaobo — were under restrictions like never before, many of them simply unable to operate, driven to poverty or inactivity because of the latest bout of state security activism. Even so, other analysts in government think tanks were more measured. Things were happening in terms of the new introductions of open governance measures, there were signs the Party elite were fundamentally revising their modes of governance and there was a sense of great internal debates in the Party that might lead somewhere interesting. Experiments in volunteering and participation at the grassroots level were offering new hope. There were even words being spoken by major political figures like the Premier at the time, Wen Jiabao, which hinted at the need for greater democracy and reform.

Of course, many of these people could invoke the detailed prescriptions that the most powerful and senior figure in the Communist Party had said at his major speech in October 2007 at the Party Congress that year. Hu Jintao, the enigmatic and largely wooden Party Secretary, had spent a great deal of time and attention in his speech on the opening day talking about the need for democracy, for taking people as the key element in society, and for introducing more participation in the whole political system. Hu's friendly words had embraced civil society, the 93% of the country who were not Party members, and the many millions who felt that they were losing out on the vast wealth creation going on around them, producing the first of China's new legion of dollar billionaires. It seemed to prefigure a new kind of politics, something unpacked in a book written by three scholars and an official at the Central Party School in Beijing which offered a detailed blueprint for reforms which did not threaten the unique role of the Party in society, but introduced new levels of transparency, accountability and efficient governance in society. [2]

At the same time as I was on this month-long tour around China, from Beijing to Shanghai, Hohhot in Inner Mongolia, then down to Xi'an to look at a neighbourhood committee, over to Hong Kong to look at the state of civil society groups under the "One Country, Two Systems" structure, another book was also circulating, operating more as a popularist counterblast to the harmonising rhetoric of a lofty, remote figure like Hu. For the authors of *China is Unhappy*, issued in early 2009, the Olympics had been nothing more than a badge of shame, not pride — a moment that celebrated China becoming the sweatshop of the world, stitched up by its elites who had marched to the orders of the World Trade Organization and the International Monetary Fund, two *bêtes noires* of the Chinese right, and who had failed their own people in such fundamental ways as not being able to produce safe food, not being able to protect against shoddy buildings destroyed in earthquakes, and basically allowing the larcenous, greedy, carnal political-business elite to grow obscenely wealthy. This book was represented as a nationalist attack on foreigners. But a more careful reading shows that it aimed most of its ire at the elite in the political centre in Beijing, the people on the Politburo crowing about harmony and taking people as the key. Wang Xiaodong and his fellow authors sounded like shock jocks from the West, their line of political complaint as visceral and entrenched as any right- or left-wing critic in a democracy.[3]

---

[2]Zhou Tianyong, Wang Changjiang and Wang Anling (eds), *Gong Jian, Zhongguo Zhengzhi Tizhi Gaige Yanjiu Bao Gao, Shi Qi Da Hou* (Storm the Fortress: A report on the Reform of China's Political System after the 17th Party Congress), Xinjiang Production Corps Publication House, Xinjiang, 2007.

[3]Wang Xiaodong, Song Shaojun, Huang Jilao and Song Qiang (eds), *Zhongguo Bu Gaoxing* (China is Not Happy), Phoenix Publishing, Jiangsu People's Publishing Company, Jiangsu, 2009.

Just as these two works occupied extreme ends in the public debate of where China should head and what its current state was, so during that visit in the summer of 2009 I was struck by how little consensus there was between the people, Chinese and non-Chinese, I spoke to. For some, reform was just around the corner. For others, this was simply the dark moment before the dawn. There were those I spoke to who were wholly cynical about where everything was heading, and pooh-poohed any suggestion I tried to make that the elite were thinking about fundamental change, and trying to embed more deeply the rule of law or modes of consultation with the public. Different notions and ideas swirled around. One prominent academic simply told me, in a noisy coffee shop in the university district, that the one thing China wouldn't stomach was lecturing from the busted polities of Europe or the US, which had just had their economies tank because of the global economic crisis. But another from a neighbouring university said that China needed the engagement and attention of the outside world, and that as long as we stuck to detailed and specific cases and didn't engage in broad ideological debate, then Chinese leaders, despite their shrill public exterior, would listen. A hardened activist based in Beijing put all of this in perspective, however, when, one rainy afternoon, he introduced me to a group of business people from a central province who had come to Beijing to seek his help after being forced out of a local village election they had campaigned in. They handed over documentation of some of their experiences at the hands of public security officials and cadres locally; who had imprisoned, blackmailed and beaten them. All this seemed a long way from the organised, measured and somewhat abstract debates that were going on across much of Beijing.

*

This book contains a series of short articles I have written, some of them in collaboration with others, over seven years from 2006 to 2013 for the Open Democracy website (http://www.opendemocracy.net/), run from the UK. I originally wrote for this site when it was edited by Isabel Hilton, the distinguished journalist and now editor of the China Dialogue website (https://www.chinadialogue.net/). The main editor I have worked with over this period, however, is David Hayes, to whom I have dedicated this collection. These pieces, on different subjects, and in different ways, present some of the perplexities and confusions of this period — they are therefore presented in some ways as a means of recruiting others into my evolving confusion. Samuel Taylor Coleridge, the great Romantic era poet, wrote that knowledge was a gradual process of admitting what you did not know and understanding limits. In that sense, these pieces are explorations of ignorance, and admissions or confessions of how great my confusion has become.

Of course, they cover the great events over this time — the Olympics in 2008, in particular, and the uprisings in Tibet and Xinjiang that year and the year after, as well as the events in Inner Mongolia which were less covered but every bit as significant in 2011. They track the fall of Bo Xilai from early 2012, and look at issues around the great leadership transition from that year and the next. They cover some international affairs, and some domestic issues, but are necessarily random and discursive. Almost all the pieces here were inspired by specific events or "trigger moments", when some kind of fond conviction or belief I thought I held about China was tripped up by encountering the more complex reality of the country. In the years from 2006 to 2013, during which I wrote these essays, I have visited China over 30 times, and been to over half of its 31 provinces and autonomous regions. I was part of delegations that met Xi Jinping, Wen Jiabao, Liu Yunshan and Li Keqiang — all of whom were, or are, members of the Standing Committee of the Party, and therefore at the summit of decision making in China. But I also met plenty of business people, academics, activists, journalist, diplomats, officials and, of course, friends. Conversations and discussions with many of these helped surrender a little more of the terrain I thought was dominated by knowledge and certainty to confusion and admissions of perhaps being wrong. This at least might help explain why the pieces may come across as contradictory. The simplest explanation for this is that even in the space of seven short years, China was a different place in 2013 to that which existed in 2006. That is how fast the pace of development and material and cultural change has been in this period.

The set narrative of this period might go something like this. In 2007, at the 17th Congress, one of the five-yearly meetings of the Communist Party saw a new line up of leaders. Hu Jintao and Wen Jiabao were still there in the Politburo, with the conservative stalwart Wu Bangguo, but there were some surprising changes around them. The dark figure of Zeng Qinghong made an unexpected exit, despite his closeness to former leader Jiang Zemin and his still being eligible to stay in the Standing Committee (he was a few months shy of the formal retirement age of 68 and so the rules would have allowed this). In his place, there came some new leaders, two of whom were lifted from right outside the full Politburo itself — the relatively youthful Xi Jinping and Li Keqiang. This was read as a clear sign of where the next leadership, due in another five years, might be heading. Analyses I read and heard at the time judged the Congress a clear victory for Hu, after five years of wrestling with the residual influence of his predecessor, the octogenarian, highly active Jiang Zemin. Finally, Hu was seen as being surrounded by his own people and able to have more space to act. Now, the sense was, we would really see what was in his heart.

We can say that over the next five years, there were two striking achievements. The first of these was the raw production of GDP growth. A businessman speaking at a meeting in Seattle in 2008 said this crisply enough: "China is a factory of GDP growth. No one can take that from it". This factory continued to spout out growth throughout the next few years, even as the rest of the world tumbled into negative or flat figures. While Europe and the US contracted in 2009, depriving China of all important export markets, it still managed to post growth figures close to 10%, largely as a result of a massive fiscal stimulus package. By 2010 and 2011, growth was in double digits. At a meeting in early 2009 in London in which the governance and political woes of China were discussed, a company representative stopped everyone dead by declaring, "Well, no matter what you say, you have to keep in mind one single thing — over 8% growth". It was a compelling figure to look at, backed up by the highly symbolic moment in 2010 when China replaced the country it had perhaps the most vexed relations with, Japan, to become the world's second-largest economy. Communist China, much press declared, was the king of capitalist-style growth, while the capitalist world was failing at its own game. This gave the space for excited talk of a China model that was now ready to be rolled out over the rest of the world.

This growth made China richer and stronger. It meant that China was able to have a guaranteed seat at any table where major global economic and political decisions were discussed. The climate change conference in late 2009 in Copenhagen would have been meaningless without the world's largest emitter of greenhouse gases there. The G20s convened over 2008 onwards were only truly meaningful because China was present. There were even those who said that the other 18 members of the group were there as a courtesy. In the end, it was G2 that mattered most — the US and China. Knowing the prickly insecure nature of the US, Chinese leaders were quick to downplay this iteration. Even so, it was proof of how China was quickly creeping into every area through its economic size.

In this period, too, Hu's leadership was able to maintain consensus, despite the historic proclivity to the Party to be riven by deep internal arguments and contradictions. Urgent attention was given to maintaining unity through ideological campaigns like the harmonious society promotion, and the scientific development concept, but also through ensuring that the elite leadership at the very top spoke and acted as one. Analysts in 2010 looked hard at things that both Hu Jintao and Wen Jiabao, as the two key figures in this leadership, said about democracy and reform during the celebrations at the end of the year of the 30th anniversary of the creation of the special economic zone in Shenzhen. They claimed some kind of fissure, with Wen veering towards more liberal ideas and Hu sticking fast to conservative ones. Wen Jiabao's article in the Party media mouthpiece, the *People's Daily*, about Hu Yaobang, commemorating the 20th anniversary of his death in April 2009, was also seen as a major sign of schism. Media appearances and the sanctioned official language used about each leader were taken as clues to their imminent falling out. But, as Party Secretary, Hu maintained a complete neutrality, using language that was overwhelmingly opaque and formal. He avoided all personal register, and perfected the art of using expressions so abstract that it infuriated even the most faithful Party member. A conversation with the International Liaison Department of the Central Committee in 2011 strayed onto this issue of elite leadership communication and the need for politicians to convey optimism, hope and mobilise the public's emotional support. Leaders at that time like Bo Xilai, the Politburo member and Party Secretary of Chongqing, were adept at this. But when the name Hu Jintao came up, a chill fell across the room. So many there had suffered during lengthy demonstrations of the Party Secretary's skill at speaking with great length and little art.

Boring the audience into profound, distracted slumbers at least maintained a kind of unity. Consensus was maintained even as the Party faced the threat in 2006/2007 of the fall of the Party Secretary of Shanghai, Chen Liangyu. It stayed in place through the uprisings in Tibet and Xinjiang, and managed to persist even as the horrors of the fall of Bo Xilai occurred in 2012. This consensus may have been built on the Party coopting or seducing people with the immense riches its political control was bringing, but, however and for whatever reason, Hu maintained this unity in a tough period. Consensus amongst the political elite and GDP growth are the two great unchallenged achievements of the period of late Hu, and they figure through many of the essays written in this book.

But they came at an immense social price, and these are the less comfortable parts of the narrative of China from 2007. To those that strayed beyond their five star hotels in the major cities, and ventured off the beaten track (and even for many of those that stayed on the beaten track, but had eyes only slightly open) China was getting wealthier but scrappier, less harmonious and less content by the day. There were statistics that tried to show this, but plenty of first-hand experiences truly revealed just how messy society was getting. In the summer of 2010, staying in Shanghai, I saw a large angry gathering outside a hospital in the centre of the city protesting about the poor treatment of a patient who had died. They wanted compensation. In Beijing, a steady stream of plaintiffs had been reduced to such levels of desperation that, when I went to visit in the same week I had come back from Shanghai, they were pleading their case outside the building housing the representative office of the UN. In Xi'an, just after this, I wandered past the vast centre for receiving petitions in the city centre — something so prominent it had its name written in English under the Chinese. All of this happened as Human Rights Watch issued a disturbing report on the treatment of petitioners who, wholly dissatisfied with their treatment at the hands of local officials, tried to plead their case with the central government in Beijing. Many of them ended up in semi-private black jails, sent back to where they had come to be beaten, mistreated, silenced or, in the very worst cases, disappeared.[4]

---

[4] Human Rights Watch, *An Alleyway in Hell: China's Abusive Black Jails*, November 2009. Available online at http://www.hrw.org/reports/2009/11/12/alleyway-hell-0. Accessed 22 August 2013.

This contentiousness in a China whose most senior political leaders were daily chanting the mantra of harmoniousness often grew tragi-comical. Landing at the chaotic Beijing airport a little before the Olympics were due to close the whole city down in the late summer of 2008, I saw two men slogging each other with their fists, shouting in rage, under a sign declaring in Chinese and English "Beijing People are Friends to All the World". Some of the violence was casual, but upsettingly common. On another occasion, a young woman passing by in central Xi'an seemed to be holding the hand of her boyfriend, but when I had walked past them I heard a loud smack, and turned to see her back away from the guy she had just struck full in the face, him holding his head in his hands looking stunned. This sense of a society of unequal wealth but rising levels of resentment and anger was backed up by the tide of social media reports showing officials going crazy when refused rights to board planes they had already arrived too late for, or of angry army leaders and their families on planes beating up air hostesses that irritated them. The most extreme cases of this heedless behaviour came from the offspring of high-level officials, stuffed so full of surplus wealth and years of behaviour that indulged them and gave them an inflated sense of their own worth that they drove around cities at such speeds and so recklessly that they knocked over and killed pedestrians and then arrogantly declared that they were above the law when taken in by security officials.

Hu's harmonious China was a place of deep ambiguity. It was a place where the world could gaze in awe on the 2008 drummers playing at the very start of the opening ceremony of the Olympic Games on 8 August that year, but where, across Tibet, despite decades of investment, building of infrastructure and political attention, a generation of young ethnic Tibetans felt so alienated and resentful of their treatment that they exploded in rage. Even the promise from the centre of more money flooding into the region from 2010 to deal with these issues did nothing to stop the tragic series of self-immolations that occurred from 2011 onwards, reaching triple digit figures by 2013. China was a rich country, where many came to make their fortune, but also a place that, despite its wealth, simply could not buy the world's love. Efforts during President Hu Jintao's visit to the US in early 2011 to have adverts in Times Square extolling the attributes of a "win win" China seemed to fall on deaf ears, with annual public opinion research surveys separately commissioned by the US-based Pew Group and the BBC, showing a mixture of admiration, apprehension, confusion and sometimes overt dislike and distrust by many in the rest of the world towards China. An experienced speaker at Chatham House in 2006 admitted during his presentation that throughout his half a century of engagement with China, it had always been a "politicised" issue. While Maoist-inspired campaigns to radicalise the rest of the developing world and take on the paper tigers of the West might have long since ceased, there was no doubt that views of China were becoming more complex and ambiguous. Chinese companies were suspected and unknown, and the shrill unease at how China was operating in the world around it was represented by works as crude as the sensationalist *China's Silent Army*,[5] perhaps the nadir of this sort of simplistic, opportunistic analysis.

The real problem with this soft power fixation by officials in Beijing was that it sat at odds with diplomatic stances from 2009 that grew harsher on issues like China's outstanding maritime disputes with its neighbours or its position on Tibet or Xinjiang. The awarding of the Nobel Peace Prize to Liu Xiaobo turned the efforts by China to let the world see it and appreciate its good side better 180 degrees the other way. While Hu Jintao and other leaders maintained their lofty, disdainful silence, Chinese diplomats throughout the developed world were faced with the undignified task of yelling at their host country governments to boycott the award ceremony. My own limited experience of this veered from the disturbing to the comical. Chinese diplomats in the UK complained about a series of defensible, innocuous events being held in Chatham House while I worked there from 2010. One on press freedom, held in collaboration with the Chinese Service of the BBC, attracted their attention because it was attended by representatives of the New Dynasty TV station, widely known to be linked with the outlawed group in China, the Falun Gong. One afternoon, I was subjected to a surreal demand by someone in the Chinese Embassy in London who demanded that, at this event on press freedom, a representative of the press be banned.

---

[5]Juan Pablo Cardenal and Heriberto Araujo, *China's Silent Army: The Pioneers, Traders, Fixers and Workers who are Remaking the World in Beijing's Image*, Allen Lane, London, 2013.

For the journalists, both foreign and Chinese, beaten up in China as the second decade of the 21st century progressed, this issue was no joke. The chief propaganda head, Liu Yunshan, himself a journalist from Inner Mongolia in his early career, where I lived in the mid-1990s, was associated with particularly hard lines on press liberty. As part of a delegation, I met Liu while still a mere Politburo member in late 2011 (to almost everyone's surprise, and perhaps most of all his own, he was elevated to the Standing Committee in 2012). Something Liu said struck me forcefully at that time:

> Every day, since reform and opening up in 1978 started, China has been in a period of change. Everything around us has changed. Sometimes we go back to places we haven't visited in China for a couple of years, and find that the whole of the landscape has been rebuilt, restructured and redesigned. But there are things beyond the changes we can see physically. There are the changes that are not visible, the changes in people's hearts.

And speaking to a people whose hearts were evidently changing almost day by day was not easy. A close friend who taught me much over this period said one evening in Beijing that the problem was the West had a century or so to undergo the social and political changes that had come about through industrialisation and modernisation. China had tried to do it in just a quarter of that time. In doing so, China has taken the full brunt of these changes. Someone aged 50 or 60 in 2010 would recall haunting experiences: from the mass campaigns and deprivations of the Cultural Revolution to the mass starvation in the 1960s. A far cry from now, a place where officials are able to order so much food at their official banquets that they are estimated to spend the full budget of the entire Olympics on indulging themselves in a single year. These 50- or 60-year-olds' lives spanned the China that was reliant on bicycles, where people needed to get approval from their work units to marry, have children, and travel outside their home place, to one where over 230 million were migrant workers living a drifting existence far away from home, and where divorce rates were sky rocketing and the youth were experiencing the same kind of sexual revolution that had occurred in the West from the 1960s.

What did people believe in all of this? When the world was going crazy around them, and public values were adapting, changing, realigning and reforming — and sometimes simply disappearing — where were people's hearts in China? Money of course was one of the great themes, with a rising obsession in places like Beijing and Shanghai first of all, but then deeper in the country in other cities with material pleasures, consumption and luxury brands. The streets were stuffed with Bentleys and Ferraris, and the high streets with Louis Vuitton and Christian Dior outlets. One businessman in Inner Mongolia thrust his mobile towards me in 2007, declaring nonchalantly that the unexciting chunk of technology I was holding had put him back over USD 10,000. The craftsmanship and of course the brand were what he was buying. Vintage wine started to find its largest market in the country, and celebrated chefs started to look at opening up concessions there. Beyond this though, the sense of a society where something had gone badly wrong with its social mores and sense of identity was clear in the appearance, or at least public recognition, of serial killers, rapists and people who were so socially isolated that they died alone and were left for weeks undiscovered. Events like the brutal manslaughter of a little girl by a truck driver who ran over her several times to make sure she was dead so he could avoid paying too much compensation to her parents sat alongside the horrific story from 2009 of enslaved farmers working against their will in mines and children sent into sexual servitude, raped and brutalised by their fellow adult countrymen who had simply lost any vision of themselves as human beings and moral actors, deepened this feeling of social moral crisis.

Liu Yunshan would never have been able to explicitly accept this, but the simple fact was that the Party could make eminent sense of the economy, thus making people's material lives better. But on the issue of where the diverse, complex citizenry of contemporary China, with their very different ethnicities, social positions, wealth levels and cultural outlooks actually located their deeper values and what pleasures they got from their new found wealth, the Party became harshly exposed. Its own history of deploying violence when in a bind was not an easy one to paper over. Historians like Yang Jisheng in his monumental *Tombstone*[6] described the horrific extent of the famines from the early 1960s, and the clear culpability of the leaders then, particularly Mao, in bringing this about. But there were endless issues about the suffering of so many in the Cultural Revolution from 1966, some

---

[6]Yang Jisheng, *Tombstone*, Allen Lane, London, 2012.

of whom were now China's most powerful leaders, and of the psychological damage done in that period. Ba Jin, who died during this period, wrote that the Cultural Revolution was a spiritual holocaust.[7] It was one, however, for which no one had fully apologised and about which there was still deep social resentment amongst those over the age of 50 in 2010. The Party was happy to allow space for people to express justifiable anger against the colonial and aggressive crimes of the Japanese, British or Germans. But the more complex issue of dealing with how the Party itself had victimised its own members and people at key moments after 1949 when it came to power was one that Hu and Wen and the leaders around them never sanctioned direct discussion of. The problem was that the Party which had changed and adapted so much after 1978 had created a society which was, in many ways, alien to its core theoretical and political values, or at least those that had brought it to power in the first place. It was a Party brought to power by revolution and violence, and now governing through wealth creation and under the veil of "consent". This was the ultimate contradiction in Chinese society. This was nicely captured in, of all places, a nightclub in Harbin, Heilongjiang in the winter of 2008 when I was being hosted by some local scholars from the Academy of Social Sciences. One of them, a congenial and friendly individual, was just about to enjoy a long sip of the beer they were holding, when I simply asked them a question that had popped into my head, "Do you believe in Marxism–Leninism?" He stopped mid-motion, stunned, his face frozen, and his mouth almost dropping open, simply unable to say anything. That moment was a kind of epiphany. The publicly stated belief system in China, it was clear, was a veneer and performance, something clothing and concealing something else. The simple fact is that, once you looked a little behind this notion, in the shadows and blurred boundaries, you started to wrestle with the real question — what was the nature of power in modern China? Power, in the end, was the concept that one had to keep returning to, to really come to grips with Hu and Wen's brave new world.

---

[7] Ba Jin (trans. Geremie Barme), *Random Thoughts*, Joint Publishing Company, Hong Kong, 1984.

*

Power was akin to a quality, something in the atmosphere or the air in contemporary China. It was well described by a journalist I spoke to during the power transition in Beijing at the Party Congress in 2012 who had been present at the Great Hall of the People during much of the 18th Party Congress that year. The odd thing, they pointed out, was the extraordinary sense of self-satisfaction and narcissism amongst the 2,500 or so attendees. They were well-dressed, well-fed, their skin almost shining with a sense of being chosen as one of the recognised elite, the club of clubs that would symbolically be present when the final summit of all this, the Standing Committee of the Politburo, was anointed. Of course, no one seriously believed that there would be any real consultation during this meeting, at least not with this group. The real decisions on the final line up and who would be in and out were being made behind closed doors, with a tiny group of real king makers (no queens in this particular line up) who were going to decide the final outcome. But the congress members this journalist had seen shone with the reflected glory of being close to such powerful people. They were, she said, "people who actually smelt of power". It was true. In contemporary China, power not only glows, but it also smells different.

Her description was a little reminiscent of the one contained in Chan Koonchung's uproarious *The Fat Years*. In his anti-dystopic vision of the imminent future (the novel was produced in 2010 and only set in 2013) the residents of Beijing are so overwhelmed by self-satisfaction and happiness that it is literally almost killing them. The carefully selected, nurtured and pampered new elite purred with a sense of material well-being, whether in designer clothes, nice new houses or expensive imported cars. Who could honestly begrudge Chinese enjoyment of their new wealth and a final glorious resolution of the horrors of their recent history? Even so, the journalist, and Chan's satirical novel, referred to an underlying sense of unease and anxiety, something that was being blocked out but still managed to rudely thrust itself in, breaking the pleasant atmosphere. This was perhaps connected to the sense of artificiality and impermanence that lurked under the surface. There was no more fitting monument to this than the horrifying and worrying statistics about the great structural challenges of China. Water, for instance. A common measure of what *per capita* water volumes are needed every year was 2,000 cubic metres. 1,000 cubic metres was danger level. Beijing managed to survive on just over 130! It was a city that was already living on borrowed time, at least on this measure. Air quality? Once more, Beijing took the lead. A standard safety measure for particles in the air was exceed by over 200 times in the city in January 2013, at the same time as the leaders were spending billions of *yuan* on imported equipment to filter the air in their offices. None of this presaged a happy ending, but almost all of it gave the wild, careering excess-driven elites with their sensational exhibitionist ways the appearance of people celebrating because time was running out.

In such a system, as many of these pieces show, power was the great constant — the one invariable. And its repository in modern China was the Chinese Communist Party, an entity that figures, directly or indirectly, in almost every sentence I wrote for Open Democracy over this period. The Party is the unifier, the one entity that spreads nationally, socially, institutionally and economically across the diverse carnival world that China has become. It was the still point in this world in which people could be libelled, cursed, even killed for falling before those more powerful or with bigger mouths than theirs. The Party guardians and agents appealed to its moral and political mandate in order to act, fiercely attacking anyone wittingly or unwittingly straying into the sacred grove of its power and challenging it. Those who I have written about here — Gao Zhisheng, Liu Xiaobo or the activist who I had known briefly in Inner Mongolia in 1994, who was then subsequently put in jail for over a decade and a half, and then released into permanent harassment afterwards — were amongst the few who openly, publicly, violated one of the greatest taboos, and directly challenged the Party's legitimacy on having a monopoly on power. Their treatment served as a warning to the curious, those who wanted to quiz or doubt the power holders of the Party. And against them, as I also write, the Party was able to use fair means and foul, to take what initiatives it wanted, to act above or under the surface, in order to protect its interests. Under Hu Jintao, as contention went up, and courts and petition systems collapsed due to burgeoning demand, expenditure on domestic security rocketed. By 2012, according to figures publicly released as the National People's Congress, the country was spending USD5 billion more on domestic security than national defence — a staggering USD111 billion. Security agencies like the Ministry of State

Security, the Ministry of Public Security and the People's Armed Police, nationally and provincially, were going through a golden age. Some of the good fortune came simply from the fact that elite leaders, despite their powers, always acted like they felt vulnerable and flustered. Tibet in 2008, Xinjiang in 2009, Inner Mongolia in 2011 and then the Jasmine Revolutions abroad, and the endless confrontations between local protesters and police all created the sense of a Party and its elite under siege.

The Party often seemed like a state within a state, with its own internal dynamics and discourse. Some compared it to the Catholic Church, others to a multinational company, driven by an internal ethos, notions of self-preservation and the need to create profit. Trying to work out what sort of thing it was took up a lot of effort and study, and never really resolved itself satisfactorily. It was only when I was travelling around Silicon Valley in California in late 2011 and visiting the great modern companies of the internet age like Facebook, Google and LinkedIn that I realised there were eerie parallels between them and the Chinese Communist Party. Facebook in particular had the same internal opacity, it seemed, the same complete focus on one strategic objective (in its case, seducing millions upon millions to surrender intimate details of their life to a medium utterly dominated by a commercially driven company) and the same reliance on a problematic but iconic founder. In very different ways, the Chinese Communist Party has also been ruthlessly focused on its key strategic objectives in recent years, maintaining GDP growth. Facebook's representative put up a map of the world on a screen for me to look at. There was its global usage, spread across every country and continent over the face of the planet, but with this vast black hole in the middle — the territory of China, where Facebook was resolutely blocked. There was little hope of the company getting across this new virtual wall for a simple reason — nothing to do with censorship itself, but everything to do with the fact that the Chinese Communist Party knew all too well that the Chinese market offered Facebook potentially massive profit potential. Why open this amazing coffer of wealth to some American outfit when you could keep it all in the family?

The Party accommodation of a system where wealth creation and money making are taken to such extremes seems, on the surface, highly contradictory. It is this paradox that many wrestle with when they look at a China where leaders mouth expressions about socialism with Chinese characteristics, but where signs of ostentatious wealth seem to hang around every street corner. Factoring in power helps get to grips with this great paradox. The Party cannot, in the end, buy the affections of the people it rules over, and perhaps does not even want to. But it can certainly buy their allegiance — at least for the moment. And the pact where people are left to make as much money as they can, and leave the power-elite to play their political games, at least superficially, seems simple enough to understand. A deeper analysis, however, shows that, in fact, the Party elite are linked to the money makers, and in alliance with them, at every level and in every possible way. Party officials might not be able to personally wallow in immense observable wealth — at least at the central leadership level. But their powers are monetarised by every conceivable kind of network around them. And in some indescribable and highly complicated but universally acknowledged way, the Party is linked intimately to the modes and means of making vast fortunes. There is an alchemy, a synergy, between the political super elite and the army of those who are getting rich, with a profound sense that in the end, what the Party can give in terms of opportunities and space to make money, it can almost instantaneously take away. The link between power and money is the great dyadic relationship of modern China, and the Communist Party the ubiquitous bridge between them. There is no other route.

*

One of the great paradoxes of trying to observe and study China during this period is to see not just how the country changes, but how views outside of it and its status have also transformed and become more complicated. It seems to me that, over the last two decades, when I read academic or scholarly material dealing with China, whether as a student, diplomat, business person, consultant or academic, that a large amount of this posited China, the entity of China, its historic experience and its language, culture and people, as something like an object of study, a kind of static "thing" in a laboratory that needed to be analysed, dissected, taken apart and have its entrails and intestines ripped out in order to fathom and then analytically describe. A lot of this attitude was simply because for many of those still around who committed to studying and understanding China from the 1950s onwards — during the period of its temporary but profound enclosure and isolation at least from the West — access to the country was hard and, for most of them, information had to come second hand, or through observation posts like the then British-controlled Hong Kong, or Taiwan. Those that managed to get decent access into Maoist China often had to make firm political pacts, which they were largely unable to stray from for many years after Mao died in 1976. Even the generation of those that were in China from the 1970s and into the 1980s were engaging with a country that, at least from many of their descriptions, seemed to be waking up from what James Joyce called, through Stephen Dedalus, the protagonist of his great masterpiece *Ulysses*, "the nightmare of history". This may have been about early 20th-century Irish memories of the trauma of freeing themselves from Britain's colonial control, but it has universal application. Restraints and clearly circumscribed no-go areas even existed when I lived in China in the mid-1990s.

That early generation of scholars and mediators of what China was and how it was developing up to the early 1980s were often marked by either political sympathy or antipathy towards what the regime in Beijing was doing, and highly limited modes of access. This latter was through no fault of their own. Many areas in China remained no-go ones for foreigners, and making friendships with local people even in Beijing was often a draining challenge, with a highly paranoid system of state surveillance in place to ensure this remained firmly under control. A tightly controlled, predictably uniform China, in which social systems, political action and governance were extremely static and entrenched, conspired to create this sense of China and the Chinese being objects for laboratory-like scientific observation and description. The position of the observer and their experiences, sympathies and proclivities was never much questioned. Atop all this sat a strong sense of China's difference, of this "difference" and uniqueness being some kind of handle on its complexity, and something that observers and those trying to understand the country could cling to. Whatever else we didn't know, we certainly knew that China was different and the Chinese were not like us. That seems to be an underlying mindset of much of the material from the 1970s onwards.

Now the carnival in China is reflected in a carnival of commentary and analysis and scholarship outside of it, produced by think tanks, universities, governments, consultancies and about every other entity one can think of. I am as implicated and embedded in this as anyone else involved. I have written books, articles, papers, essays and short pieces like the ones gathered here about China, adding to this mountain. I think now, however, that there is a wider acceptance of the subjectivity of those that observe, and the ways in which this inevitably conditions what they see and how they see it. Chinese ideologues at the Party School to this day like to rail against subjectivism, so I suppose it is best to qualify that last sentence by an admission that while I am sure there is a world out there separate from us that we can see, and ways which are more or less accurate to describe what we see, at the end of the day this is a complicated process with no easy routes. In these pieces, therefore, I have implicitly and, towards the end, explicitly accepted my culpability and agency and the evidence of my subjectivity in what I try to describe and see.

During the Beijing Olympics I was struck by how polarising debate at that time was, particularly over the torch ceremony and the clamour about China's human rights record. Whatever the validity or otherwise of the specific claims about China's state behaviour in this area, the more general point was that people at that time with no evident prior interest in the country, no ability to speak its language and often no experience of even having visited the country physically, had strong opinions either for or against it. In one debate in London during this time, a journalist linked to the Marxist party of Great Britain, while mangling the names of Chinese leaders, blasted back at someone who had attacked China over its role in Africa by a coruscating attack on the UK and its colonial role in the past. One academic in attendance wearily admitted after this clash that these debates were as often as not about ourselves than they were about the country we were meant to be talking about.

I could work up a certain level of smugness and complacency thinking of the ways in which I had learned Chinese, lived in the country for over five-and-a-half years, been reading about it up to PhD level for almost two decades, and, from my first visit in 1991 to 2012, I had visited China over 80 times. I was fond of bragging to people inside and outside China about how I had visited every single autonomous region and province, from Tibet to Sichuan, Gansu to Shaanxi, Heilongjiang to Jiangsu. But the question kept on recurring, as I went through more debates and discussions like this, where China became increasingly like a concept or a notion, battered between two sides for one of them to try in the end to take control of it and assert some sort of strange intellectual hegemony and dominance; was I really engaged in anything any better? I might have read more, experienced a bit more and engaged a bit more in China as it existed now than many of these, but at the end it was only a matter of degree — I was trying to appropriate and nail down some concept of a country, its culture and people, despite the fact that this was evidently impossible. More often than not, deeper reflection showed me the China I was trying to speak about was my China, a Chinese conducive to me, the one I went in search of the moment I arrived, a China which was compliant and in accordance with my inner wishes and interests. I was quick to get irritated by Chinese officials, for instance, talking about their China, despite the fact that, in all sorts of ways, they had more right to speak and more validity about what this "China" was than me; a non-native, non-resident, and someone who was, in the end, an outsider.

While these essays have been grouped thematically, they have also attempted to map this very personal journey, and to plot out the ways in which I have had, intellectually and emotionally, to be open about admitting my own self-interest and self-incrimination. Whatever has been written here, much of it during the immediacy of events or issues about the country China both internally and externally over the period 2006–2013, has to be read with an acceptance that these are pieces by a person brought up in the English educational system, who started off reading English literature at Cambridge and only wandered, almost by accident, into an engagement and interest in China in the very early 1990s while living in Japan. I only learned Chinese as a language when I was in my mid-20s, and then pursued largely an accidental career, first as a teacher in China itself, then as a business person, then as a diplomat and finally as an academic. This hybrid path helps perhaps to explain some of the hybrid perspectives that are given here. It is hard to think of someone who had worked purely as an academic or a diplomat taking a similar position.

Nennius, a writer in Britain in the ninth century, wrote in his fragmentary history of the country that "I have made a heap of all that I could find".[8] The matter in these pieces is to make some kind of picture, not particularly scientific, and often largely descriptive and impressionistic, of China as it

---

[8] Nennius, *History of the Britons* (*Historia Brittonium*).

has undergone transformations and changes that at least mattered to me in the period over the late 2000s. This was for many a perplexing period, some of the contrariness of which has been alluded to above. In all of this, there was something strange about the figure, in particular of Hu Jintao, who seemed to epitomise the enigma of China. Those I knew who had met Hu were consistent in saying just how controlled and like a scholar or an academic he seemed. And yet, ostensibly at least, he was accountable for a system which was still deploying distressing levels of coercion and violence, one that seemed unable to deal with the figure of Chen Guangcheng, the blind activist who, before his exile from China in late 2012 was the subject of intense levels of harassment and official surveillance in his home town of Linyi, Shandong province. Why was it that, in a case that was causing China major problems with its international image, not one of the central leaders showed any interest in getting involved in it? Were they in fact not so powerful at all, and incapable of moving against local officials? How did one then explain the ruthlessly efficient way in which they ordered the removal of Bo Xilai? And why did Hu remain silent and remote even when the government and Party were being attacked for their actions in Tibet from 2008 and their behaviour over the imprisoning of Liu Xiaobo in 2010? Did he simply not care about the damage these issues did to China outside, or did he not know or not understand? Was he badly advised, or operating from some profound conviction that the Party could exercise power the way it liked, and these people deserved what was happening to them?

Any visit over this time to China, at least for me, was transformative in different ways, showing new aspects and new ideas about what the country and its people were becoming. For all the many stories that were worrying, upsetting and concerning, there was also daily evidence while there of the extraordinary dynamism and energy of the country, of the many people who were living the kind of lives they wanted to live utterly away from any form of State or Party involvement, of wonderful anarchic spirits, and people who conducted themselves with inspiring dignity and thoughtfulness. For as many people as shouted and pushed themselves around publicly to show off their sense of importance and power, there were vastly more that acted with wit, humour and self-deprecating dignity. The most remarkable moments were when, unexpectedly, common ground was found through humour and a shared sense of the rich absurdity of daily life in Carnival China — officials who had a glint in their eye as they blasted out wonderful stretches of Hu-style empty rhetoric, roaring with knowing laughter when congratulated on their verbal ability, or taxi drivers whose interest in where you were from became irrelevant when on the shared subject of the humiliations of having two national football teams as ontologically wired to deliver disappointment as those of England and China. It made little difference where people were from in China, the good humour was widespread, a nation of wags flexing their skills on the Chinese social media or in public, embracing the irony of what China under market socialism and harmony was becoming. For the author of these pieces, therefore, China was never, and could never be, an object of study, but more a constant source of enrichment, stimulation, perplexity and inspiration, a place where one went to engage profoundly and always in ways in which one came away changed. As the quotation at the start of this introduction stated, a carnival is not a spectacle seen by the people but something they live. The China here is not an object or a spectacle either, but something in which I, and the people I write about and engaged with over this period, lived and changed. That was Carnival China in the first years of the 21st century, hurtling towards a new and unique form of modernity, one in which it was not only changing itself, but changing the rest of the world.

Chapter One

The Context: Governing China

In 2011, I made my first visit to Russia. It was strange having spent so much time in China, a country evidently profoundly affected by the Soviet Union experiment in governance, to finally come to the true spiritual home of this system, despite the fact that it had collapsed over two decades before.

At a meeting with an academic based in Moscow and specialising in Asia we got onto the subject of governance in China. I ran through a long list of challenges that I felt faced the country — the over-mighty powers of Party Secretaries in townships and counties upwards, their lack of accountability, the ways in which local strongmen were beginning to reappear, running mafia-like organisations in some parts of the country, and the frequent clashes between officials and the people they were meant to serve. The Russian academic looked at me sourly as I ran through this grim menu, then gazed out of the window and said, "Well, here in the Russian Federation we would say China was pretty well governed. Have you tried to get anything done in Siberia or elsewhere outside the main cities in this country? I think you'll find China is a doddle compared to the grief you'll have here."

This Russian interlocutor had a point. The Chinese Communist Party had searched its soul since the failure of its Russian counterpart in 1991, and come back to the issue again and again, trying to learn lessons from why the Soviet experiment had not succeeded. Party School thinkers, academics, officials and even foreign advisors had all been recruited in a massive consultation process to set out the key things that the Soviet Union Communist Party had done which the Chinese one needed to avoid in order to survive.

By 2007, the Chinese Communist Party looked in robust health. There were no other real sources of political competition, and even the slightest sign of defiance in society was met with brittle and intolerant brutality. The China Democracy Party which briefly flared into life in Hangzhou and other provincial centres in the late 1990s was snuffed out in a matter of weeks, its two dozen or so leading lights given lengthy prison spells. Being a member of the Chinese Communist Party came back into fashion, with membership climbing into the 70-million mark in the late 1990s and, a little after 2007, passing the 80-million mark. But working out what sort of thing the Party was for outsiders proved challenging. It was not a political party in the usual sense, more a universe all of its own, with internal procedures, a mini culture, codes of behaviour, and a tight core of secrecy at its centre around two key things — its budget and the way it made key appointments across society. To this it added information control, though that particular area became a bigger challenge as the decade wore on.

This chapter begins with analysis of the expectations around the 17th Party Congress in the Autumn of 2007. Party Congresses held every five years in China are always a big deal — the core set pieces of Party management, and the biggest clue to its vision for the rest of society through the main speeches its highest leaders make. This particular Congress was anticipated because of the clue it was meant to give to the leadership which would be in pole position when Hu Jintao and Wen Jiabao were due to retire in 2012 and 2013.

The 17th Party Congress was also significant because, as many commented at the time, it marked the period when Hu Jintao was meant to be his own man. This was discussed in the Introduction. Those expectations towards him were perhaps exaggerated. He worked within a group of leaders, tightly interlinked and circumscribed, where the notion that someone might be able to push forward policies and campaign on their own was next to impossible. This lack of political space became clearer as 2012 approached, with Hu widely interpreted as failing to get his key protégés and supporters into the next Standing Committee. From 2007, what was more striking was the ambiguity on the part of the Party — the way in which on the one hand it supported bold initiatives like the Open Governance Law of 2008, allowing citizens access to government information, yet on the other hand clamping down on rights lawyers and civil society activists, or the ways in which it liberalised some areas of the economy and allowed greater freedoms to non-state business people but also tightened its control over the banking and finance sector. At the same time as China was opening itself to the world as never before with the Olympics of 2008 and the Expo in Shanghai of 2010 (see Chapter Two) it was also pouring resources into the state security apparatus as never before. It was no wonder that observers found China deeply confusing over this period — a confusion reflected in the pieces on the role of the state and the Party in this section.

China's 17th Party Congress: Getting Serious

5 October 2007

The "17th National Party Congress" in the People's Republic of China hardly sounds like an event that merits front page headlines far outside Beijing. Nor, on past precedents, will the gathering in the Great Hall of the People on 15–19 October 2007 see much in the way of visible drama. On the contrary, the images beamed to China's own people and to the world will be familiar, as lengthy speeches from the rostrum will be delivered in front of the serried, impassive 2,217 delegates from across the People's Republic of China. Some will be wearing their colourful "ethnic minority" dress, some scribbling on the sheets of paper before them, some sipping from their small cups of tea, some even appearing to be in a deep slumber.

The choreography of political transition will also be routine. Towards the end of the week of meetings, the newly "elected" top-level leadership of the Chinese Communist Party — and therefore of China — will troop onto the stage from behind a curtain. Hu Jintao (President) and Wen Jiabao (Premier) will occupy the first two slots, as they reach the second term in their respective offices. But look around them — for here is the reason why the 17th Congress of the Chinese Communist Party is worth attending to, even (perhaps) worth one or two headlines. There, beside Hu and Wen will emerge the figures that will compose the new leadership of China for the next five years, and have a chance to shape its course for far longer.

As they stand silently in front of the flashing light bulbs and the obedient applause of the assembled cadres, China's people and the world will also have the first tangible clues about who may be in the best position to replace the current "fourth-generation" leadership, which will come to an end in 2012 at the 18th Party Congress.

The national and international context China's rulers find themselves in helps to fuel intense speculation about who will follow Hu Jintao and Wen Jiabao and in which direction they will take China. It is the openness of the current intra-party situation, and the fact that there are real choices to be made, which is striking. Hu Jintao's elevation (which occurred in 2002, and signalled the gradual erosion of his predecessor Jiang Zemin's power) seemed preordained from as early as 1992, when he returned from four years in Tibet; at the time Deng Xiaoping, paramount leader in the 1980s and early 1990s, made it clear towards the end of that period that Hu had his imprimatur.

Today, there is no one with anything like Deng's political capital to set the seal on a leadership succession. Instead, there are a group of politicians in their late 40s and 50s, each of whom has a reasonable chance of stepping into Hu's and Wen's shoes. This makes the Beijing Party Congress of October 2007 the first big step on the path towards supreme power in China. Those likely to move into leadership positions at the conclusion of the Congress broadly divide into two camps. On one side, there is what may be called the "elitists": those with impeccable familial links to the Party (such as current Trade Minister Bo Xilai and Shanghai Party Secretary Xi Jinping, both princelings whose fathers were famous Party leaders). The careers of this group have mostly been spent in the booming coastal regions, or in the central government. The Party exudes from every pore of their bodies; they live and die for it.

On the other side is a less well-known group who may be called the "popularists". It is represented by people like Liaoning Party Secretary Li Keqiang, and the mayor of Chongqing (the world's most populous city), Wang Yang. These leaders have their roots in the less developed western regions of China, have worked their way up through Party organisations (such as the Party Youth League), and have had limited exposure to Western countries. In educational terms, this group has a more mixed background than the engineers who compose the entire current Standing Committee, many of whom studied in the Soviet Union; a number of the "popularists" have politics, management and law degrees, and their doctorates mostly come from Chinese universities.

What makes the outcome of the contest between these two groups compelling is that China now has real choices to make, and this means that who is in command will have important consequences for the country's direction. The challenges facing the new leadership will put the Hu Jintao–Wen Jiabao period into a different perspective. Their era seems likely to be remembered as an era of "muddling through" in political terms. Political reform has remained where it has been since 1989: off the agenda. Instead, economic development has continued to hold the limelight.

China is poised to overtake Germany to become the world's third-largest economy and (by 2010) the world's largest trading entity — both within the term of this Congress. Among the policy problems of this success that will face the country's new leaders are China's severe environmental problems, hunger for energy supplies, and need to radically reposition its economy away from the current (manufacturing-intense, export-orientated) model.

The predicament of the current and forthcoming Chinese leadership is both in the scale of the domestic issues it must address, and the fact that these are emerging at a time when China's role in the world — from Sudan to Burma — is being increasingly questioned.

The build-up to the Beijing-hosted Olympic Games on 8–24 August 2008 connects these two dimensions in a potent way. The glare of global publicity and attention is on China in a way that is both unprecedented and impossible for the Chinese government to control. There is at least a distinct possibility that far from enhancing China's international image, the government's defensiveness and mishandling of foreign journalists will turn the Olympics from being a showcase of China's new enhanced global status into an exposure of how far it still has to go.

The domestic difficulties crowding in on the Party leadership are well-documented; they include its degraded environment (which has suffered most from three decades of breakneck industrial development), increasing social inequality, corruption, and the need for financial-sector reform. The post-Congress strategy will be to follow the example of the 1980s, when Deng Xiaoping set out the broad parameters within which China would develop: encouraging a stable and benign international environment, while working to manage and improve China's internal coherence and strength.

The international difficulties are highlighted by the eruption of dissent in Burma, a neighbour of China with whose military regime Beijing has close economic ties. The crisis in Rangoon raises the question of how much China is willing to do in the interests of preserving international stability. In protecting its own economic and strategic interests, China — for very different reasons to Western liberal democracies — does not wish to see instability in the region.

Thus, it is prepared to forsake sentimental attachments and use its considerable influence to bring countries such as Burma and North Korea to the negotiating table. If its interests (energy supplies, political reliability) are under threat, it is willing to apply behind-the-scenes pressure, and if necessary threaten to withdraw support. The political elites in North Korea or Burma know that China's abandonment of them would be devastating, which may be a factor in their own search for unlikely allies elsewhere in current straitened circumstances.

Whatever the leadership in China looks like after the 17th Party Congress onwards, it is certain that the policy directions they take will affect the rest of the world more than ever before. Global economic growth, especially in light of a potential US downturn, is more dependent than ever on China's performance. The controversy over the quality of Chinese exports in the food and toy sectors (to name only those) has itself confirmed the degree of interdependence between China and the world, which makes disengagement on either side — as would have been an option in the past — unworkable.

In this sense, the faces who will step from behind that curtain during the week of 15–19 October in Beijing will be those of genuinely global leaders. The rest of the world need to learn about them: their track record, their ideological leanings, their intellectual capacity, their interests. Will these new standing-committee members finally be ready to grapple with China's greatest challenge of all: political reform?

The elitists and populists have many evident differences: from attitudes to the role of foreign investment in China, to the country's global conduct. But one thing unites them: a desire to see the Chinese Communist Party stay in power. How they seek to ensure this, and how the rest of the world responds to what they do, will be one of the key themes of the coming decade.

China's Tiananmen Moment: The Party Rules

3 June 2009

Zhao Ziyang was the General Secretary of the Chinese Communist Party when the student demonstrations in Beijing that reached their tragic dénouement on the night of 3–4 June 1989 took place. He was the most senior figure to lose his position as a result of the events, being placed under house arrest until his death in 2005. Even the announcement of his demise was low key. For these last 16 years of a long career he remained a sensitive if near-invisible figure in Chinese politics: someone who embodied the terrible conflict of conscience consuming the Party about how it should deal with the students in Tiananmen Square.

But fortunately for history — if perhaps less so for the Party — Zhao managed to record on cassette tapes over 30 hours' testimony of the heady weeks leading up to 4 June 1989. These were discovered after he died, and smuggled to Hong Kong. There, in the former Party head's own voice, is the story of the Party wrestling with what came to be called the "revolt".

Zhao's tale, now set out in the book *Prisoner of the State: The Secret Journal of Zhao Ziyang*[1] is both riveting and sobering. A key factor governing his own fate is that because Zhao had spent most of his career in the provinces, he lacked patronage at the centre: when the crunch came, he was vulnerable. He was head of the Party in name only. The real head, Deng Xiaoping, was able — once he had been influenced in that direction by others — to seal his fate in a couple of meetings. The archaic ways in which China conducted affairs, on an almost tribal model — even as late as 1989 — is staggering. So much for the rule of law!

Beyond the personal fate of a senior leader, Zhao Ziyang's account offers an important political assessment of the course of events that followed former Party chief Hu Yaobang's death on 15 April 1989 and funeral a week later — even though he does not make it explicit. It seems that in mid-April there was a good chance that the initial grievances of the students and their demands for more openness could have been met, and the entire protest peacefully defused.

An editorial on 26 April 1989 in the *People's Daily* — interpreted as the definitive voice of the Party — scuppered this with a clear condemnation of the students as agents of "chaos" and "conspiracy"; this served only to make many of them more unbending in return. Zhao contends that the villain in

---

[1]Zhao Ziyang, *Prisoner of the State: The Secret Journal of Zhao Ziyang*, 1st edition, Simon and Schuster, New York, 2009.

this respect was the then Premier, Li Peng, who may well have acted with the backing of the more conservative elements in the leadership to exacerbate the troubles and bring things to a head rather than calm them down (as he tried to do in his remarkable meeting with the students on 19 May 1989). Perhaps this is a little too Machiavellian and imputes to the "leftists" more strategic coordination than they had in reality; but during a time of such intense crisis with huge implications, the argument has to be taken seriously.

Zhao could perhaps be accused of being naïve and idealistic. In the end he was very much the product of the system that was to eventually turn against him. But his later years of being a captive of the state brought him closer to the realisation that without fundamental political reform, the foundations of China's economic prowess would always be shaky. This alone, as the considered opinion of someone who once sat in the all-important Standing Committee of the Politburo as well as being head of the Chinese Communist Party, is very significant.

Zhao's reflections on the course of events of April–June 1989 raise various "what ifs". In the end, what happened, happened — though the fact that June 1989 is still so sensitive in China shows how much of a stain it has left. In some ways, it can be interpreted as the moment when the Communist Party, rather than the government, confronted a play-off between its rhetoric on opening up and what it actually intended to do. For years it had surfed around with the ideas of freeing up civil society, the media, even village elections (which started in the early 1980s). But when the searching questions were sharply posed in 1989 about how the Party (at least for the elder leaders) might respond to proper dissent, there was only one response: the gun. It was a brutal reminder that, for all the warm words and cosmetic changes, the heart of the Party was unchanged. In 2009, is the same still true?

Probably not. For one thing, the elders have all gone now. The Party under Hu Jintao (a man like Zhao with more experience in the provinces than at the centre) is not beholden to any one supreme leader. Its tribalism persists, as does its instinct to remain in power. But the idea it could spill blood is now not tenable. If 1989 was repeated, the Party would be finished. It knows this, and therefore has undertaken massive (and exhausting) pre-emptive actions against any potential threats. The China Democracy Party in 1998 lasted a matter of days, and was crushed brutally. The same has been true of any other force from the Falun Gong to any separatist parties that have got in the Party's way. Since 1989, the key has been to stay on top of any protests and maintain political traction before they come near the level of 1989.

At the same time, talk about democracy and democratisation has become more urgent and focused. Hu Jintao famously used the "d" word more than any other in his speech at the 17th Party Congress in October 2007. The state council even issued a paper on democracy in October 2005, which says: "Democracy is an outcome of the development of the political civilisation of mankind. It is also the common desire of people all over the world."[2]

But the nagging suspicion remains that the nice talk solves nothing: the issue of what the commitment of the Party to "democracy" means is as unclear as ever. If — just if — there was concerted opposition today, as there was in 1989, how would the Party react? What would it do? How would it behave if it came to a moment when its rhetoric was finally faced with unavoidable demands?

We don't know, and perhaps that moment will never come. Perhaps the Party will succeed in its long transition to a form of democratisation that it feels comfortable with. It would be an enormous challenge fraught with difficulties. But in view of the Party's record of facing down impossible odds and coming through, only the most purblind would put its chances at nil. With such an outcome achieved, 1989 would then seem very different: not a near-death moment for the Party, but a time when it looked into the eyes of real opposition; learned how to face it down, and more — learned to reinvent itself and move on, stronger and tougher.

China's Shadow Sector: Power in Pieces

17 September 2009

I spent the month of August 2009 travelling around China and looking at the state of democracy (in the sense of "village elections"), the rule of law, and civil society. It was a sobering experience full of disturbing revelations.

---

[2] *Building of Political Democracy in China*, issued 2007, Preface, State Council Information Office. Available online at http://www.china.org.cn/english/features/book/145941.htm. Accessed 7 October 2013.

There was an inauspicious moment on the very day of my arrival, when Xu Zhiyong — who heads Gongmeng (Open Constitution Initiative), a small legal-aid NGO — was detained for "non-payment of taxes" (the grey zone in which independent NGOs exist in China means that this charge is often a convenient pretext for official persecution). Xu Zhiyong was released on 23 August, but may still face prosecution. The pattern of harassment is consistent: on 12 August a court case involving the environmental activist Tan Zuoren in the south-western city of Chengdu was conducted so badly that his lawyer burst into tears.

Ai Weiwei — the designer of Beijing's Olympic stadium (the "Bird's Nest") and one of China's most prominent intellectuals — had travelled to Chengdu hoping to testify on Tan Zuoren's behalf, but to no avail. There was a chilling sequel: Ai was rewarded for his efforts by having his hotel door hammered on in the middle of the night, then — when he opened it to see what was going on — being punched senseless.

The current political atmosphere, if anything, works to diminish attention to such incidents. The approach of another important anniversary — that of the founding of the People's Republic of China, on 1 October 1949 — heightens sensitivities about internal stability. The riots in Urumqi and elsewhere in China's western province of Xinjiang in early July 2009 have made the government, and the ruling Communist Party, even more nervous than they were already.

Indeed, in interviewing people from various organisations and from very different perspectives, I was struck by a consistent undertone of worry about the prospect of a regime change (even a "colour revolution") along the lines of those in the post-Soviet states in the early 2000s — which culminated in the governing communist or reformed-communist parties being ejected from office in elections. China's clear official aim is to ensure that it doesn't make the same mistake. But in a country undergoing rapid change, how much of the political course of events and outcome can the Party still control?

The leading Party ideologues issued a booklet on 5 June 2009 called *The Six Whys*,[3] in an apparent effort to bolster the organisation's ideological armoury in the face of mounting social and intellectual challenges. The

---

[3] *Liu ge Weishenme (The Six Whys)*, People's Daily Publishing House, Beijing, 2009.

fifth item of this list was "Why a Western-style democratic parliamentary model is not going to work in China". The framing is significant: these key Party thinkers have worked out their reasons carefully for what they *don't* want to do. Their argument is that elections as they are conducted in the West would create instability; impede China's development at a critical juncture; and, in a complex society already stretched to the limits in terms of regional and class inequalities, risk the release of divisive political forces. In this coldly realistic approach the Chinese Communist Party might have a point. For, even in my brief and inevitably partial month-long journey, I was startled by how many village-level areas were lawless, ruled by different groups and largely out of the reach of the central authorities.

In China's north-east, quasi-mafia groups have made entire rural areas their fiefdoms, which they run according to their extensive business interests. In the south-eastern province of Fujian, similar elite economic groups have established control of villages via local representatives who ruthlessly pursue the groups' private interests with no regard for broader social goals. In the central provinces of Hunan, Henan and Hebei, most evidence I saw showed a clear battle between Party operatives and other increasingly powerful groups (from specific clans in one area, to economic or ethnic or social groups in another). Such tense and uneven situations help put in perspective Hu Jintao's emphasis, in the aftermath of the Xinjiang disturbances, on the need to have "one law for everyone".

In large swathes of the Chinese countryside, there seem to be as many different rules as there are groups. The strongest are taking what they want. The problem of this messy and fearful social landscape is reinforced by the Party's domination of the political landscape and the pitilessness with which it has exercised this domination. It remains the case that on many key issues, no voice except that sanctioned by the Party can be regarded as legitimate. But in many areas, it is clear that a by-product of this chloroform — namely, the attempt to be all things to all people, to accommodate (and thus internally defuse) all sorts of opinions and attitudes amongst Party members — has had the opposite effect to that intended: it has created an entity with potentially dangerous internal divisions.

Several academics I talked to offered sharp insights into the Party's and government's current predicament. One as good as said that democracy at the village level had made things worse. Another complained that lawyers were now becoming a huge enemy within, challenging the government and starting to articulate demands that were becoming more and more political in their complexion.

Behind all of this is the immense security apparatus that the Chinese Communist Party now relies on for so much for its authority in "difficult" areas. A recent report estimated that China had no less than one million secret-intelligence operatives. How are these tasked and funded; who are they answerable to; how is their effectiveness assessed? These are not simple questions to answer. But somewhere, on someone's budget sheet, are the costs of a huge amount of people assigned to use government money on "dealing with subversive and terrorist activity". It would be fascinating to know just what this amounts to in financial cost alone.

I am more disheartened than I was even a month ago by how things are in China. The central state seems less effective and less in control in many more areas that I had thought. Its responses to potential threats are becoming more and more predictable: imprisoning, intimidating and coercing. One case in particular haunts me. Gao Zhisheng, an activist lawyer based in Beijing, who had represented the legal rights of some followers of the dissident religious group Falun Gong, was prosecuted in 2006, and then put under semi-house arrest. A few dozen of the million "agents" mentioned above had been allocated the job of simply watching his house at all hours. Some had taken to following his daughter to school, even intimidating and scaring her. This is all eloquently recorded in Gao Zhisheng's memoir, published in 2007, *A China More Just*.[4]

While in detention in 2007 and 2008, Gao was badly tortured. In one report, a secret policeman is said to have told Gao that as he had written so much about what Falun Gong followers had suffered, "now he can see what it is really like". Those that met him afterwards said he seemed broken by the experience. But he did make one attempt to get out, with his wife and (now 15-year-old) daughter; they succeeded in fleeing to Bangkok, but Gao himself was arrested at his home in Shaanxi province on 4 February 2009. Nothing has been heard of him; Chinese government officials, at least in Beijing, seem no wiser than outsiders about his fate. Those who have followed the case for a long time fear the worst: that one of the million

---

[4]Gao Zhisheng, *A China More Just*, Broad Press USA, New York, 2007.

agents could have taken things a little too far, resulting in Gao's "accidental death".[5]

The courage of individuals like Gao Zhisheng in standing up for at least some concept of justice is inspiring. Even institutionally, the Communist Party has created a monstrous problem: a massive, largely unaccountable, avaricious and often ineffective security apparatus full of individuals with no legal accountability, who most of the time — at both national and provincial levels — act to preserve their own narrow interests, and who, when threatened, expertly play a "protecting-national-stability-and-interest" card. It is clear that there is only one man who can hold this massive hidden sector to account: not the head of the government, Wen Jiabao, but the head of the Party, Hu Jintao.

In light of my month's tour, the one suggestion I would therefore make to Hu Jintao as soon as the 60th celebrations of 1 October 2009 are over, is simply to look long and hard at the effectiveness, and the accountability, of this enormous undergrowth of "intelligence agents", and to ask aloud whether they don't belong to the Chinese Communist Party's traumatic past, when it was a threatened, underground organisation, rather than to its present, and future, as the ruler of a sovereign nation which now has the world's third-largest economy.

Then, after 60 years in power, the Chinese Communist Party can start to remove from the state's books some of the thugs, hard men and criminals it employs as "secret-service personnel" and see how they fare in making a more honest living in the non-state sector. That truly would be something to celebrate.

China: Inside Strain, Outside Spleen

25 March 2010

The top leaders of the People's Republic of China only very rarely make themselves directly accessible to questions from journalists, local and international. The rare exceptions include the press conference that

---

[5]Gao was subsequently seen in 2010. See Chapter Five.

concludes the annual meeting of China's National People's Congress, when the responsibility falls to the incumbent Premier.

It is not always the easiest experience, either for the Premier or his interlocutors. Zhu Rongji, Premier from 1998–2003, was one of the more accomplished performers; his blunt responses when challenged about the social pain from the huge lay-offs from the state-owned industrial sector earned him respect. Zhu was one of the few Chinese modern leaders who might have survived unscathed the interrogation of an acerbic Western interviewer. Most of the others appear to regard even the milder challenge represented by the equivalent of China's parliament as an obligation to be endured.

The current Premier, Wen Jiabao, lacks Zhu's flair. But his performance before a horde of journalists on 14 March 2010 at the end of the National People's Congress was confident and impressive — indeed, a reminder of his political pedigree in the higher echelons of China's Communist Party. This, after all, is a man who stood beside then Party Secretary Zhao Ziyang in the days of May–June 1989 which had been so challenging for the leadership, witnessed his boss going into Tiananmen Square to plead vainly with the protesting students to disperse, and survived the crushing repression that consumed Zhao's political career as well as the lives of many young people.

What was striking about Wen's presentation was its frankness about China's currently febrile social condition. He even went as far as to acknowledge that a perfect storm of inflation, social injustice and official corruption could threaten the state's hold on power. A single figure illustrates the point. China's military spending indeed increased by 14% in 2008–2009 (as the US is keen to highlight), which brings the total to over USD80 billion; but, less recognised, it has spent a similar amount on internal security. China's growing armed power may be very much on the minds of the international community — and more so with its regional neighbours. But its internal police, security personnel and legions of informers are costing almost as much.

Here, in the starkest terms, is the dilemma of a ruling Communist Party that sees itself beset as much by fear of enemies within as of enemies without. Here too is a perfect rebuttal of the notion — assiduously promoted by its official discourse — that China in 2010 is anywhere near a "harmonious society". It costs billions of dollars in hardcore security to buy that "harmony". The treatment of independent voices such as Liu Xiaobo and Gao Zhisheng is one indication of how unsettled the Chinese state is by challenges to its authority. A day after Liu was given an 11-year sentence on 25 December 2009, a government advisor and scholar of the Chinese academy of social science offered a lengthy and valuable insight into how the state views such challenges. Yu Jianrong declared that China was beset by three kinds of "mass incidents":

- Events provoked by legal grievances, where recourse through the courts and authorities had failed; most of these were about tax or property issues.
- Events provoked by the behaviour of officials, police or security personnel, which often erupted out of control and involved large numbers of citizens.
- Events characterised by Yu simply as "chaos": opportunistic explosions led by underground or hooligan elements in society.

Yu Jianrong estimates that in total there were 90,000 incidents across these categories in 2008–2009. The huge number helps explain why the enormous security budget is felt to be needed: both to contain the expressions of grievance when they become visible, and then to prevent them spreading. Wen Jiabao, of all people, knows how protests that start as small and modest (as in Beijing in spring 1989) can spread with astonishing rapidity across the country. And Chinese people in 2010 are unimaginably more integrated, more networked and more technologically sophisticated than they were 21 years ago. This Premier needs to have nerves of steel just to be able to sleep at night. This degree of ferment in Chinese society, and the lack of legitimate outlets either to express or to respond to it, helps explain why China's stance in the international arena has of late appeared more belligerent than at any time during its "peaceful rise".

The issues of trade, currency, climate diplomacy, military growth and cyber-warfare are but some of the areas where China seems to have adopted a more militant attitude towards its international partners and rivals (principally, though not exclusively, the US). There was some excitable talk at the National People's Congress about China's need for decent aircraft carriers to allow it to expand its naval capacity and thus challenge the US and others around its immense territorial waters. During the conference too, a key official in China's propaganda department responded to Google — which in

January 2010 decided to stop complying with China's censorship demands over its Chinese-language search engine, amid concerns over cyber-theft — by saying in effect that foreign companies that "didn't abide by Chinese laws" could get out of the country. That indeed seems to be what Google is now preparing to do.

The economic friction between the US and China has generated much heat in 2009–2010 over protectionism and currency revaluation; but again a single remark from a senior figure said more about China's current political mood than numerous policy papers or official briefings. The remark came from China's Trade Minister Chen Deming, who on 21 March 2010 showed a capacity for plain speech that Zhu Rongji himself might have recognised: if there were a trade war, said Chen, the US would lose.

China's more combative public rhetoric is, in light of its relatively low diplomatic profile during the years it was accumulating huge trade surpluses and high growth-rates, somewhat disconcerting to its erstwhile allies in the new "multipolar world". But seen in the context of China's internal social strains and imbalances, the discordance begins to make greater sense. A country of protest and dissent, instability and dislocation, where key institutions — the courts, banks, security services, local and national government — are being stretched as never before; a state of increasing impatience and ill-temper which ferociously denounces anyone who strays into territory — capital punishment, political reform, international trade, Tibet and Taiwan and Xinjiang — that it regards as its own business. These are two sides of the same *yuan* coin, intersecting narratives, parts of the same immense and uncertain process that is China today.

The key dysfunction in this period of extraordinary challenge for China's leaders is between economics and politics. In economic terms, China has a functioning model that is able to deliver the goods to its citizens in a way impossible to conceive of at the beginning of Deng Xiaoping's 1978 reform programme. But, politically, the system is an anachronism: unable to deliver justice, accountability or a voice to its citizens.

At some level, China's leaders know it; they are using every resource at their disposal to keep things under control. But the prickly, aggressive mood is worrying. Liu Xiaobo tellingly writes in one of his essays that this is a country where the President, Hu Jintao, cannot permit even the mildest fun to be poked at him in cartoons. He and his colleagues are trying to look far, far stronger than they actually are or feel. They are powerful, yet trapped. In many ways they deserve sympathy, even pity — though it is all too revealing of their plight that they would meet the offer with scorn.

Chinese Democracy: The Neglected Story

6 April 2011

The Chinese government continues to react uneasily to the spread of news about the waves of popular protests and near-revolution in North Africa and the Middle East. This meant that the usual nervousness around the convening of a major meeting in Beijing was even more in evidence during the annual meeting in March 2011 of China's parliament, the National People's Congress.

Teng Biao of Beijing University and other academic lawyers were detained without explanation; more controls were imposed on websites, with any news of potential demonstrations that could be interpreted as echoing events in the Middle East being quickly blocked; foreign journalists trying to cover some of the small protests that have broken out within China were manhandled, and in one case badly beaten.

The current Beijing leadership's term in office is approaching its end. In 2012, the 18th Party Congress will ratify the choice of the elite which replace Hu Jintao (President) and Wen Jiabao (Premier) and govern for the next five years. What is striking is that during the Hu–Wen years it seems that things have become more, not less, repressive. China has in the last decade grown both richer and far less at ease with itself. The country's wealth has not made its governing elite feel secure with even the mildest forms of public protest. Local officials in particular react vigorously to the possibility of petitioners ending up in Beijing, humiliating them in front of more senior leaders by pressing for their cases to be resolved. At some times and in some places, the "countryside" in China is far from a place of tranquillity and natural peace. It is instead tough, rough and frightening.

This year's National People's Congress heard the Politburo's seemingly most liberal voice, Wen Jiabao, talk with almost staged precision — both in his government work report and press conference afterwards — of the need for deeper and quicker political reform. He had made almost exactly similar remarks in 2010. A few days before, however, a fellow Politburo member, Wu Bangguo, had offered a very different political prospect. Wu spoke of the need to resist political reform, refuse any talk of multi-party democracy, and preserve stability at all costs. The fact that he is one of the body's most conservative figures, and in fact senior to Wen, indicates the extent of the ideological fissures at the top of the Party.

Yet it may be precisely because of these divisions that one of the bolder political experiments of the last 30 years, village elections, has stayed relatively static. Elections in which there was a choice of candidate, and secret ballots, have been held since the mid-1980s in China. A formal law in 1987 allowed for their expansion, and the final law in 1998 prescribed their role for the rest of the country. The experiment has not been a complete success: one activist I interviewed in the summer of 2009, when recalling a celebration the previous year on the occasion of the tenth year of country-wide village elections, said it felt more like a funeral than a party.

In the late Jiang Zemin era, there had been hopes that village elections were about to be extended to the next level of government: towns. A few townships in developed areas and in the western region of Sichuan held open elections. Much like with village ones, there was no question of these involving multi-party candidates. But there was at least awareness that these elections might improve the governance of particular areas by holding officials accountable and giving the public some say in their removal if they proved no good.

After all, at its earliest inception the belief was that village democracy would help deliver more credibility and stable governance to parts of the country that had suffered near-anarchy during the Cultural Revolution which started in 1966. It then proved a means for officials elected by public ballot to acquire a certain mandate in collecting unpopular taxes and imposing unpopular measures like the "one China" policy.

But elections did not extend to townships, and the few that had occurred were halted a year or so after Hu Jintao replaced Jiang Zemin. For Hu, the main objective was for the Party to deliver accountability to itself through the mysterious concept of "intra-party democracy". There is widespread scepticism, however, that the Communist Party can be its own "policeman", and in 2010 talk started again of the more developed areas on the coast, in particular introducing elections for mayors, and even for Party positions.

So far, nothing has happened. That is probably because, as one commentator in China told me in 2010, the introduction of democracy this high up in the governance system would have serious ideological implications, and would be vigorously opposed by the more conservative elements of the elite. Wu Bangguo's comments reveal the persistent deep unease over even the role of the non-state sector in China's economy. Any move to introduce popular mandates for town leaders would risk this spreading up to the provincial level, and then to the central government itself.

In turn, the impact of such a process on the Chinese Communist Party's monopoly on power would be profound. In the current environment there is no figure in the Party's leadership, not even Wen, ready to promote a policy that might have an unpredictable outcome. So for the moment, the status quo reigns. The repression of the last few months is on the surface disheartening. But it does also show this is a society undergoing huge growing pains, but very much in a major transition. Things can't stay as they are forever. Some kind of accountability and mandate needs to be available for local, and national, officials. Lawyers have an increasingly important role in Chinese society, and jailing the ones that deal with sensitive cases is as much an admission of panic and defeat as anything else.

Village elections might be interrupted, but they still play a big role in the way that the Beijing government brokers governance deals with perhaps the most difficult sector of the population — farmers. Moreover, at least half of these elections have been successfully conducted even amid massive restraints, which gives pause to those who continue to say that China is a society without any potential for or tradition of democracy.

Most media attention continues to be on the elite leaders in Beijing, and their condoning of the attacks on civil society leaders and legal activists. But this leaves the real story out of sight — in the vast swathes of rural China, where the impact of high growth has been divisive, uneven and in many places destabilising. The economic battlefront more often than not remains the Chinese cities, but the political one remains as it was in the Maoist period — the countryside. Here, the need to develop forms of governance that move away from coercion and repression towards consent is one of the biggest challenges facing Beijing's governing elite.

China, the Party-State's Test

3 November 2012

The state in China is an integral part of just about every major issue in the country, from its stock market and outward investment to its domestic economic development and social ferment. It's clear that exploring any of these matters in detail requires study of the state's role. Yet as soon as the point is raised, things start to become confusing. For what *is* the Chinese state?

It would be convenient to imagine that some mighty brain exists in the centre of Beijing, dictating all parts of the country's internal and external policy. But that notion is hard to square with the existence of so many contradictions, where (for example) one part of the machinery adopts an aggressive stance towards Japan over the Diaoyu (Senkaku) islands and another, a placatory one. How can such messiness be reconciled with the idea of a unified central mind or network? Perhaps the latter is playing games with itself, or trying to confuse, or is it just that outsiders are simply failing to divine its deeper intentions?

A more prosaic answer to the original question is that the true face of the state is in fact the Chinese Communist Party — and more precisely, the current nine-strong Standing Committee of the Politburo. We know, somehow, that these men (as they all are at the moment) personify and guide the state, insofar as anyone does. We don't know clearly *how* they guide it — how, for example, they instruct government or executive organs, but we sense that there is enough noise and bustle around them to confirm that they are the ones in control, insofar as anyone is. We can try to look into the shadows around them as well; but these are, after all, shadows, and once beyond the Politburo we move quickly into even more speculative territory.

But this party-state is also a mystery to those working for it. It empowers and fells people in ways which are hard even for its intimates to unravel. They too must speculate, and read the atmosphere — as when on the final day when Bo Xilai, hitherto one of the elite's most powerful figures, must have known that the air around him was poisoned and that the very entity he had worked most of his life for was about to abandon him. There is an echo here of the Mao Zedong era, when those desperate to beg for the leader's intercession knew there was no hope when calls were not taken and doors were closed in their face. But in that period, everyone knew the state and Mao were in effect the same thing. These days, the powers of the state — and the variety of unwritten rules — are more elusive and dispersed; when you have fallen foul, there is no way to appease them all. The greatest task of a modern leader in China is to try to enlist to his side enough of these influences to be able to do the job.

Now, with the imminent Party Congress in Beijing, the process of leadership succession which has unfolded over several years is reaching its climax. From within, it was probably far harder — in its lobbying, struggles, pressures and feuds — than those outside the inner sanctum can ever know (though the Bo Xilai affair gives a dramatic taste). Behind the froth of highly orchestrated mass meetings and (the few) public events and pronouncements, this has been overwhelmingly a campaign conducted in private meeting rooms and closed sessions.

That fact alone, however, poses a huge legitimacy issue of the process and its outcome. Elections, in the end, answer complex, even tedious questions in an easy way: who gets the most votes wins. In this opaque Chinese version, the emergence of the next party-state leadership leaves everyone else wondering: why and how were the contenders and the winners chosen, what are their qualifications and qualities?

On the one hand, the party-state wants to surround itself with as much mystique as possible in order to preserve its monopoly on power. On the other hand, it needs to tell some sort of story about why the new leaders have arrived in their position and what distinguishes them. It can't, moreover, just answer by saying they are the best-networked people in the Party or have the most support from this or that faction. The party-state has to spread out its arms and show — or at least pretend to show — that the new leaders are there not just for the Party, or for the State: they are there for everyone.

It is almost 70 years since Karl Popper published his 1945 work, *The Open Society and Its Enemies*.[6] The operation of the party-state in modern China exemplifies its theme in raw form. If modern China is about anything, it is about the fight for control — information control, social control, political control. The Chinese Communist Party has won this battle so far by pouring

---

[6] Karl R. Popper, *The Open Society and Its Enemies*, Routledge, London, 1945.

huge resources into all of these areas. It has been able to continue doing this because of the country's vast GDP growth, which has meant it can pursue every other area of activity at a discount.

This is bound to change, in that growth will increasingly come through greater efficiency, and that will require both better governance and management, and fundamental political choices. There will need to be more consensus not just amongst the political elite but in society. To use or allow violence to quell disputes or protests, for example, will become counterproductive. The Party will need to persuade people's hearts as well as capturing their bodies. It will wrestle with the same issues of meaning, value, lifestyles and expectations as developed societies. It will need a new vocabulary beyond the idea of economic success as the summit of human existence. It will have to look at the world beyond GDP, and deliver more to its citizens than the possibility of becoming richer.

These are great challenges, arguably bigger than any the Chinese Communist Party has faced before. It's hard to imagine the controlling figures that will appear on the stage in mid-November either being bold enough or having the capacity to meet them. And yet, the future of this great country, with its energy, complexity and dynamism, also seems to demand an effort on the same scale.

Chinese people are like people anywhere. In the end, they want to live in a country where they feel secure, fulfilled and hopeful; a country where they can aspire — perhaps even dream — and strive for a better world. That might at present be more a proposition than a detailed programme, but an open society — a society with less restraint and fewer controls — is the only way to make it happen. That is why the development of China is such a critical part of the story of humanity and its fight for openness, justice and equity.

Chapter Two

Society in Carnival China: The Beautiful,
the Damned and the Olympics

China had won the bid for the 2008 Olympics in 2001, right at the end of Jiang Zemin and Zhu Rongji's period in power. The night on which the announcement of their victory was made by the International Olympic Committee, Beijing almost exploded with the fireworks set off to celebrate. It was one of those rare moments when the glee of the elite leaders and the public seemed to be as one.

Securing the Olympics was Jiang Zemin's achievement. Delivering it would be Hu's. But, in hindsight, despite the fact that so many pieces in this chapter concentrate on the expectations of the Olympics both inside and outside China before it happened, and then on assessments of what the event had actually achieved afterwards, the Games themselves with their drama and bombast grow less important as time goes on. There is no more poignant symbol of this than the somewhat desolate monuments erected for the Games, in Beijing in particular, some of them standing wholly unused and in the early stages of decay just five years after the Games ended.

Chinese leaders talked of the Games being about "One World, One Dream"; and this became the slogan attached to the campaigns leading up to them. But what was clear throughout 2008 was that this moment when China was about to reveal its great achievements in rebuilding and reacquiring what it thought was its historic status was not reciprocated in a particularly straightforward manner by much of the rest of the world. The torch ceremony, weaving its way across the planet, became an event ensconced in celebration and criticism in equal measure, with some nasty conflicts in France and the US. The net effect of events around this torch ceremony was to remove many of the more benign ideas about China that many Western observers had until the summer of 2008. For many Chinese, there was resentment at what they saw as the ill grace of outsiders not entering into their moment of glory. For critics of China, within and without, it was just this sort of event that showed the arrogance and hubris of Chinese Communist Party rule. Parallels, unfair in many cases, between the infamous 1936 Olympics in Berlin and Beijing were made all too easily. Perhaps the greatest impact of the Games was the way in which they deepened and made more complicated the dialogue between China and the rest of the world. From 2008, there were no more excuses for easy answers or simple narratives. China was part of the world in ways it had never been before and had a right for space and respect, and the rest of the world had to think of a future where a place with such a different political culture and outlook was integral to almost all major global decisions.

The more significant moments of 2008 were not those that happened in the Bird's Nest stadium, partly designed by Ai Weiwei, who was himself to be crudely detained and bullied only a few years later. The uprising in Tibet in spring of that year, the vast and tragic earthquake in Wenchuan in May and June which killed tens of thousands of people, and the collapse of Lehmann Brothers bank which truly ushered in the global financial crisis in September had more profound and longer-term impacts. Tibet was a rude awakening, something which will be discussed in Chapter Five. It struck at the heart of the legitimacy of the party-state and does much to explain the onset of more elite leadership anxiety and sanction of repressiveness subsequently. The Lehmann Brothers demise threw wholly unexpected challenges at China's economy into 2009. In this context, the August 2008 celebrations were an isolated moment of distraction.

Shanghai: Formula One's Last Ride

15 October 2007

Shanghai lobbied hard to get the right to host Formula One. The city sent letters and delegations to the office of Bernie Ecclestone, and even had to fight off a counter approach by the inland city of Xi'an. Its persistence was rewarded. In 2003, it held the first ever race, on a brand new, state-of-the-art course. To Shanghai, it was another symbolic advance in its long campaign to become *the* modern city of Asia.

Formula One should appeal in China. Like the bustling, hectic life on the streets, it's a sport without pause or reflection. The noise and power of the cars act as a metaphor for what China, and Shanghai in particular, has become: non-stop juggernauts of growth, leaving trails of smoke in their wake as they forge ahead. Socialism, at least in Mao Zedong's and Deng Xiaoping's China, was always about progress, hurtling forward. It appeals to the Chinese that Formula One cars never go in reverse.

The circuit is an impressive sight: an hour's drive along newly constructed highroads from the mighty Bund in the centre of the city. Shanghai, with 2,000 skyscrapers over 20-storeys tall, might be one of the most densely populated places on the planet. But at least out where the racing is, there is some open space. Like the skyscrapers, what might take years to build in the West was put together in a matter of months. Even four years on, the place looks like it was opened yesterday. The grass still looks like it is getting settled in. There are a few immature trees. The buildings by the track still have the smell of plaster, concrete and paint.

It wasn't ever very likely that a project this size, involving this amount of money, was going to avoid the great endemic of modern Chinese public life: corruption. In September 2006, the number one Communist Party official in the city, British-educated Chen Liangyu, was felled for involvement in massive graft scandals involving housing and pension funds. But everyone knows here that he would have only sat at the tip of a very large iceberg. Under him were hundreds of thousands of other officials and business people up to every imaginable scam. After the fanfare of the circuit opening, therefore, the usual rumours of impropriety circled around. The track had been built with dirty money, and gained by backhanders, favours and graft.

That might account for the lack of politicians at the Formula One track in Shanghai during the Grand Prix on 5–7 October 2007. Party officials are always eager for the chance to leave their prints over any event, no matter how seemingly low profile it might be. Formula One is a big deal, a sport with a global audience and massive media coverage. But Shanghai's two leading political figures — its new Party Secretary Xi Jinping, and its longer-term mayor Han Zheng — are nowhere to be seen, either during the practice days or when the big race itself starts. For once, it seems the threat of reviving claims of corruption has preserved the sport from the sort of political manipulation that afflicts everything else in this city and country.

The result is to give the 2007 event an oddly genuine international feel. There are no opening declarations from red-festooned podiums by leaders with fiercely slicked-down, dyed hair; no ribbon-cutting ceremonies, with *qipao*-clad young women draped around impassive-looking senior Party officials; no resounding words of praise for a "more open, more prosperous, more developed China". There is only the briefest playing of the Chinese national anthem as the cars rev-up and get ready on the starting grid. Then a nervous pause, as a few of the English-language banners imploring Lewis Hamilton or Fernando Alonso to win flutter amid specks of rain in the slight, pre-typhoon breeze, before the cars tear away.

Shanghai's attentions, like China's generally, have been refocusing around the gigantic, global event of the Olympic Games in Beijing on 8–24 August 2007. But the city is also already looking beyond, to its hosting of the World Expo on 1 May–31 October 2010. Formula One is hardly on the same scale, but even with the job well done it may strike the Chinese attending that, with no Chinese driver, it's not after all really "their" sport; more just another piece of Westernisation they feel they need to buy into, but nothing that, in the immortal words of Mao Zedong's wife Jiang Qing (in talking about revolution) "touches the soul".

The impression is reinforced by the visual contrast between (on one side) the cavalcade of phenomenally well-paid drivers, technicians, car-company executives and corporate guests and (on the other) the hordes of people who line the roads towards the circuit holding out forged tickets, parking permits and pit-stop tags. At a slightly further distance, the peasants working on nearby fields appear quietly indifferent to the astounding parade of wealth and privilege.

Perhaps the peasants are right. China, indeed, would never have got anywhere without their back-breaking labour in the early years of the reform period; and today, the surplus labour from the farms now moves into the cities to build the mighty skyscrapers that are coming to dominate the urban landscape. They, along with many members of the new Chinese middle class in the city, must wonder whether all the effort, investment and work to get Formula One was really worth it.

An indication of the ordering of the event is that the evening headlines on the night of Lewis Hamilton's sudden exit focus not on the race but on the "Special Olympics" being held at the same time. In some ways,

Shanghainese have moved on before Formula One even had a chance to arrive.

Beijing's Political Tightrope Walk

13 March 2008

China's Premier Wen Jiabao has said that he is the world's most worried man. Across his desk pass reports on the many issues that could endanger the country's stability and halt its steady growth; among them, environmental damage, energy supply problems and social unrest. At night, in the peaceful seclusion of the central Zhongnanhai compound next to Beijing's "forbidden city", the worries must, if anything, intensify. Wen's years as a consummate political insider and survivor may have brought him to a commanding political position, but nothing can have prepared him (or indeed anyone) for the task of steering the mighty entity that the People's Republic of China has become on a stable and sustainable course.

The Premier's annual report to the National People's Congress (which on this occasion met in Beijing on 5–18 March 2008) is a regular fixture in the Chinese calendar. It can also be supreme political theatre. In the days of Zhu Rongji — Wen's predecessor in the 1990s — the wily, brilliant Zhu would swipe away pesky questions with a dazzling insouciance that enthralled visiting foreign journalists. Here was a man consigned to forced labour in jail in the 1950s for being a "rightist", subsequently rehabilitated, and now with little left to fear. As a journalist friend said to me in Beijing, there will certainly never be another Zhu. It's an impossible act to follow, but Wen has been doing a good, competent job; lower profile, but respected and reasonably popular.

That is, until the snowstorms and associated energy shortfalls of late January 2008, which left the government in chaos and provoked significant disgruntlement among Chinese citizens stranded in the attempt to travel home for the New Year. The worst winter weather for decades left millions stranded at the worst possible time. China's migrant workers — the very people whose loyalty the government of Hu Jintao and Wen Jiabao have tried so hard to enlist and secure — were left to languish in railway stations throughout China's coastal regions. This combination of elements — a large, prolonged public assembly of Chinese wage-earners denied a rare chance to see their families — came dangerously close to igniting the social tinder box that the Chinese government spends a huge effort day after day seeking to contain.

The government belatedly went into crisis mode. Wen even presented himself to the throng gathered at Changsha station in central China — voicing concern and even (in an unprecedented gesture) apologising on behalf of the government. Xi Jinping, elevated to the Politburo at the 17th Party Congress of 15–19 October 2007 (and a favourite to be China's next President), was dispatched to the poor province of Guizhou to express contrition.

Those less on-message received a scolding. The central government sternly rebuked the leadership of Yunnan (south-western China) for its inefficiency in the face of the weather-induced travel chaos. The widely reviled Jia Qingling, head of the Chinese People's Political Consultative Conference, also became a target when, in preceding Wen at the National People's Congress meeting to deliver his work report, he largely ignored the travel problems and offered no explanation for the failures of China's disaster planning — attendees and delegates openly criticised him.

Wen Jiabao's own report to the National People's Congress was important less for the mantras about "thought liberation" and breaking "the shackles of old ideas" than for a more prosaic reason: his setting of targets both for economic growth and for inflation. He has already been criticised for over-optimism in these areas, and this criticism was itself a signal of the nervousness of the political climate.

China's current inflation rate — the consumer price index rose by 8.7% in February 2008 and food costs rose by an astonishing 23.3% — presses greatly on its people's livelihoods. In the popular mentality at least, the two things that combined to destroy the legitimacy of the nationalist government that fell in 1949 were inflation and corruption. In truth, the forces leading to the communist takeover were larger: most of all the country's utter devastation by 12 years of war, both internal and external. But no one can dispute that by the end of the regime's life, a ruined economy — to which spiralling inflation had contributed — meant also an exhausted government that had lost the love of the people.

In 1989, the same coupling of corruption and inflation was a factor in the disturbances that so unsettled the Party (albeit these factors were overshadowed by more directly political ones). In the mid-1990s too, the inflationary spectre required adept intervention (a famed "soft landing") by then Premier Zhu Rongji to cool the Chinese economy. More than a decade later, the problem looks more intractable, and Wen's annual inflation target of 4.8% seems ambitious.

The rises in the price of meat and other staple foods (some of them steep) make living conditions tougher for the very constituency Hu and Wen must keep happy — farmers, migrant workers, factory workers; that is, the billion Chinese not yet part of the burgeoning middle class the post-1978 reforms have created. For these people, every *yuan* matters. The budgets even of urban dwellers are stretched to the limit. They are already saving furiously to cope with a host of responsibilities: health costs, housing costs, the educational costs of their children, the growing number of older folk in their families, as well as unexpected emergencies. In these circumstances, a hike in food prices is very unwelcome to people all over China. For the Beijing leadership, inflation much beyond 5%–6% could become a major political headache, and Wen's crisis management crash course during the deep freeze would prove to be only the precursor to a much harsher sequel.

All of this makes the billions of dollars spent on the Olympic Games look increasingly incongruous. The main buildings are finished, and Beijing is now attending to the details. But the cold international atmosphere — assiduously reinforced by campaigners who have sought to brand the extravaganza as the "genocide Olympics" — has exposed the Chinese leadership's obvious lack of preparation in the arena of images as opposed to infrastructure. The reaction in China to Steven Spielberg's resignation from the creative committee of the opening ceremony — both defensive and insinuating — is demonstrative of a deeper confusion. Despite seeking counsel from Western public relations firms, Chinese officialdom still has a long way to go in dealing with a story-hungry, fractious and sceptical foreign media that is very far from the pliant creature it is used to at home.

Thus, the great event of 8–24 August 2008 — far from being the smoothly spectacular entry onto the global stage that Beijing envisaged — is shaping up to be a big test for the Chinese leaders. The problem for Hu Jintao, Wen Jiabao and their comrades is that the international spotlight on their hosting of the Olympics (with all the criticism this entails) requires them to show to the Chinese people that they are standing up strong and proud for China's interests at the very time when they must (in jittery economic circumstances) continue to deliver the all-important growth that they need to remain secure in power.

True, they are tough and realistic people, and are probably in as good a shape as any rival elite would be to meet the challenge. But they face a balancing act as difficult as any that will earn gold during the Games; and if the leaders get through reasonably unscathed, they will merit a place on the Olympic podium for political acrobatics.

China's Olympics: After the Storm

6 May 2008

In hindsight, it can look as though China's apparently tortuous last six months have been part of some masterly public relations (PR) plan to manage the world's expectations of the Beijing Olympics. The problem was that these expectations were becoming dangerously high. A PR campaign was, then, required; its purpose was to reduce them to such a low level that even a moderately well-run event with no major calamity could be portrayed as a success. The strategy of the Chinese government — and its key PR advisors, Ogilvy and Hill & Knowlton — was to arrange a succession of events that left the rest of the world in awe.

The sophisticated campaign comprised four stages. First, there was the circulation of claims — increasing by late 2007 — that China's nefarious role in the western Sudanese province of Darfur was guaranteed to make Beijing the "genocide Olympics". This argument culminated in February 2008 in the resignation of Steven Spielberg as creative director of the Olympics' opening and closing ceremonies (though on this last point, the Chinese government could preserve the appearance of wounded pride by pointing out that there was nothing for Spielberg to resign from as he had never signed a contract). Second, there were the uprisings in Tibetan-inhabited areas in mid-March 2008 — from the Tibetan Autonomous Region itself to Sichuan and Gansu — which led to the death (according to Tibetan accounts) of over 100 people. These had been preceded, and were followed, by incidents of protest (including demonstrations) in the north-western province of Xinjiang. Third, the Olympic Torch's global procession faced vocal demonstrations in a number of Western capitals, which degenerated into scenes of chaos as Chinese defenders (mostly students) of their country's right and dignity clashed with Tibetan activists and Western human rights protestors. Fourth, China has continued its squeeze on its own internal dissidents; the three-and-a-half-year sentence handed in April 2008 to the internet and environmental campaigner Hu Jia for crimes of subversion is only the most visible of many examples.

This storm of bad news for the Chinese government was as unexpected as it has been unremitting. In such periods, its leaders will often invoke the advice of the classics — in this case Mao Zedong himself: that the best way to deal with defeat was to use it as a basis for the next victory. When its ferocity has subsided, the nine-strong Politburo — in place only since the 17th Party Congress on 15–19 October 2007 — may well observe the becalmed landscape and come to see the storm as a blessing in disguise. As long, that is, as the tumult really has ended.

The People's Republic of China, and the Chinese people as a whole, have shared with many people outside China a set of inflated, unrealistic notions about what the Olympics could or will deliver. When Beijing won the right to host the 2008 Olympics, many people on all sides may well have sincerely believed that in seven years' time China would have made great progress both in human rights and in political reform. Their hopes proved unfounded, but their optimism should be no more dismissed than others' bleak (or in this case realistic) pessimism deserves to be applauded. After all, both attitudes are almost equally well grounded in relation to the history of the People's Republic of China. Any informed observer can easily demonstrate that the country's record over the 59 years of the state's existence is a mixture that can incorporate both. It is likely that that will always remain a predominant reality in a country as multilayered as China — and it will, no doubt, be a recognised part of the assessment of the Olympics when the curtain falls.

Here, then, is the beauty and sophistication of the Chinese government's six-month PR plan. Now that so many voices have interpreted the string of crises and challenges facing Beijing as auguring disaster in August, this outcome has — almost by default — become much less likely. The combination of protests and tensions have reminded people of a reality that is often half forgotten: that China has a dark underside, and that its gleaming modern cities in the coastal areas are only part of a much more complex social story.

The 30,000 journalists heading to Beijing will be more than half aware that many of the "undesirables" (beggars, prostitutes, migrant workers and dissidents) of the "modern" People's Republic of China will have been removed from the city. They will know that they are looking at a highly stage-managed event. This will represent both a significant departure from the triumphalist and celebratory fixations of the pre-disorder period, and a prophylactic against the potentially much worse story of armies of foreign journalists being shocked by what they discover. The news management — and the "disillusion" — has already happened.

The Chinese government, then, has managed to observe a classic rule of any good PR campaign: get the bad news out first, and give yourself time to deal with it. The government may have looked surprised when the outbursts happened in Tibet, and the turmoil there does indeed raise serious questions about their handling of this and other "minority" regions. But Beijing can face these at another time and place: it would have been far worse for them if Tibet had exploded just before, or — even worse — during the Games.

The government can also rightly point to the fact that the whole torch-ceremony fiasco was not its own idea, but a daft leftover that, in its present form, dates only from the previous Olympics, in 2004. And it can use its experience of the Olympics to demonstrate to Chinese people a conclusion many of them have already reached: namely, that when China eagerly embraces a Western idea or product — and then actually lands it — there always seems to be a sting in the tail.

Marxism–Leninism led to revolution, devastation and near implosion. Western-style industrialisation has led to the near-annihilation of the Chinese environment. China's 21-year hunt for a Nobel Prize was rewarded first in 1989 by the awarding of the Peace Prize to the Dalai Lama; then in 2000 by the awarding of the Prize in Literature to the obscure émigré Chinese novelist, Gao Xigjian. China's "Nobel fever" was cured after that, and there is general indifference each year to the decisions of the various committees, now regarded as bribed and biased insider groups.[1]

As a result of these experiences, China may well be further emboldened to go its own way. The Olympics has been a final opportunity to see that these symbols of Western development are not so great. But China now has stakes in some of the great symbols of the Western corporate world, such as Merrill Lynch and BP. China is starting to push back. Many young Chinese know that the likeliest outcome for the short- to mid-term future is for Chinese companies and organisations to initiate a fresh and startling process of globalisation. More and more of the international agenda is now in China's hands to shape.

So, as Western journalists write the Olympic stories they had already planned months before, delivering them to an audience who are already suspecting them — and thus deprived of their element of surprise and shock — the Chinese people, like sensible people anywhere, will be relaxing, sitting back, looking at this event and seeing it for what it is — a mere three weeks of corporate frenzy, redeemed by a few sublime moments of sporting excitement, which will dissolve almost as soon as it is over. When it is finally over, the Chinese people will be able to continue the remarkable journey they began many decades ago and which, unlike the Olympics, really can and will change the world.

China on Olympic Eve: A Globalisation of Sentiment

11 July 2008

The long march to 8 August 2008 is nearly over. In less than a month the opening ceremony for the Olympics will start. Now is a good time to look at where China stands on the eve of its great showpiece and how the jamboree might take its part among the events of this already tumultuous year in influencing China's relationship with the world.

---

[1]A sentiment only reinforced by Liu Xiaobo's peace prize in 2010, but partially cured by Mo Yan's one for literature in 2012. See Chapter Five.

China in 2008 has already lived through a series of extraordinary events: dramatic, tragic and unexpected. No one anticipated the explosion of anger in Tibet and the neighbouring areas in March–April — least of all, it seems, the Chinese central government — and no one foresaw the great earthquake on 12 May 2008 in south-western China that claimed the lives of over 60,000 people.

These two events, in very different ways, capture the fragility of modern China. This great economic juggernaut that scares and worries so many people outside the country contains within it deep weaknesses and problems. The protests in Tibet showed that the diverse ethnic mixture that lives within the current geographical boundaries of the People's Republic of China exists under an uneasy sort of truce that is inflected at every level by historical and political issues.

The modern China that came into existence in 1949 is overshadowed by a host of previous "Chinas", which together are radically different to the current one in size, ethnic mixture and stability. These Chinas have left profound memory traces. Tibet is only the most prominent; Xinjiang, Inner Mongolia, even Yunnan — as well as other more profoundly Sinified provinces — also contain echoes of that diverse and disunited history. The events in Tibetan-populated areas are a sharp reminder that many people — inside and outside China — take the modern country's unity too lightly at their peril. Chinese dynastic history over the last two millennia has been a cycle of fragmentation and disunity followed by centralisation and strength. This history may grow silent, but it never goes away; the latest generation of Beijing leaders, in their reaction to the problems in Tibet, showed that negotiating in ways that compromise Chinese unity is not on its agenda.

The earthquake raises more complex issues. The history of devastating natural calamities in China is a long and terrible one. Earthquakes in the Ming dynasty (1368–1644) wiped out whole cities and regions, killing hundreds of thousands. Floods carried devastation even further; the Yellow River was even called "China's sorrow" on account of its history of destroying whole communities through the centuries. Typhoons, droughts and tidal waves have all taken their toll. The political role of these events has sometimes been dramatic, with dynasties and states ended by the final onslaught not of man, but of nature.

The highly rational, scientific and atheist membership of the Chinese government supports active campaigns against superstition and cultism. But there is a question here over how far its campaigns reach or can reach today into the hearts of the Chinese population. To many, this recent series of disasters, man-made and natural, looks inauspicious and ominous. The members of the Politburo may be obliged to project a look of outward strength, but there are many ways in which politically they have to treat every day as though it were their last. Why else would Premier Wen Jiabao quite sincerely describe himself as the world's most worried man?

John Keay, in his narrative *China: A History*,[2] writes of the attempt in the late Song period (11th century) to create political associations that reformed and opened up the Chinese political elite from one-man absolutism. A scholar of the period, Ouyang Xiu, attempted to convince the reigning emperor of the need for tolerance of political factions and organised interest groups. This idea was rejected. A contemporary scholar of Chinese imperial history bitterly noted: "China still struggles with the heritage of this 11th-century political failure."[3]

This suggests that even in 2008, many negative phenomena in China have deep historic roots; and that being aware of this at least helps both to put events in perspective and to interpret them with a degree of balance. In this light, for example, the disappointment Ouyang Xiu must have felt after his learned recommendation was turned down can be seen as just one distant antecedent of the anger of many Chinese bloggers today at the corruption, complacency and greed of the government and its agents. But in this too, discontented Chinese citizens (bloggers or otherwise) may have much more in common with their counterparts in other parts of the world than many may think. Publics around the world — in the US and Europe, in the Middle East and India, in China itself — are all, it seems, fed up and disillusioned by our politicians. We are — especially in these times of economic stress — impatient with them, frustrated by their inability to deliver the simplest things and irritated by their boasts. If the Chinese past and the Chinese

---

[2]John Keay, *China: A History*, Basic Books, New York, 2011.

[3]Fredrick W. Mote, *Imperial China 900–1800*, Harvard University Press, Cambridge, Massachusetts, 1999.

present are connected in multiple ways, then so in this sense is the Chinese present connected with that of its national equivalents across the world.

This "globalisation of sentiment" as it might be called is, too, part of the reality of things on the eve of the Olympic Games. If people on all sides can begin to understand how much this experience connects rather than divides them, then the celebratory Olympic slogan "One World, One Dream" may begin to acquire some more meaningful reality. The sight of George W. Bush and Hu Jintao standing next to each other on the podium may even reinforce the sense that these elite figures exist almost in another universe, without real accountability to their peoples. In any case, we are about to find out. China's year is about to become even more interesting, more globalising and more surprising.

The Olympics Countdown: Beijing to Shanghai

5 August 2008

The Beijing Olympics opening ceremony on 8 August 2008 is now in sight. The final rehearsals are underway; the Torch nears its final destination; display boards and the front pages of newspapers feature clocks counting down the hours; the stringent security checks at the airports are in place; a few protestors who managed to get visas are protesting. The sign at Beijing airport proclaims the official message of controlled harmony as well as the Olympic slogan, "One World, One Dream".

Yet even now, on the eve, not everyone is included in the embrace — or rather, it seems, wants to be. A horde of people the authorities regard as unsightly has been cleared from Beijing's central streets and neighbourhoods as part of the city's ferocious clean-up campaign; and there is heightened surveillance and monitoring of potential sources of disruption, internal and foreign. The welcome to some visitors, not just the protestors, is less than warm: Lorna Ball, the head of the BBC's Chinese service, found herself abruptly disinvited to the opening night.

Many long-term foreign residents are leaving Beijing voluntarily for the duration. The climate makes August a hot, hard month in the city anyway; and the first eight months of the year have been full enough of nationalistic jubilation. True, tickets for the events themselves have been hard to get.

But hotel rooms, it seems, are not a problem — the 60%–70% occupancy of three-star premises in Beijing is actually *lower* than usual for a peak-season month. So much for the panicky warnings to book rooms in 2001, the moment Beijing won its bid.

A few days in Shanghai also offers a refreshing take on the Beijing razzmatazz. China's second city is oddly underwhelmed by the imminent epoch-making festivities in its great rival to the north. The waterfront Bund is being dug up, in order to install an underground road tunnel so that the area can be pedestrianised. This will take until 2010, when the city has its own great event — the Shanghai World Expo on 1 May–31 October. The most that this proud and sophisticated city will get from the Beijing Olympics is a few football games. It's hard not to feel that most people here are going through the motions, without real enthusiasm.

The reverberations of events in China's south-west and north-west have reached its east. The explosions on two buses in Kunming, Yunnan province on 21 July that killed two people and injured 14 created nervousness, though officials denied claims by a Xinjiang separatist group that it was responsible. The attack in the city of Kashgar in Xinjiang itself on 4 August which killed 16 policemen heightened the tension. In the aftermath, the head of Olympic security appeared on TV and in newspapers solemnly declaring that the threat is real and that people must be "vigilant". I asked a friend in Beijing about plans for the opening ceremony: "I could have got a ticket," was the reply, "but I'll watch it at home. It's too dangerous." If this is how nervous an everyday Chinese citizen feels, then it is hard to imagine what President Hu will be going through.

The first arrival of sportsmen and sportswomen happens at the same time as the journalists. It's hard to work out which group is more important to this event. Until now, the sport has seemed like an afterthought. When logging onto the internet, the arrivals discovered quickly that a lot of sites were blocked. True, last-minute negotiation between the International Olympic Committee (IOC) and the Beijing authorities led to the unblocking of some of them. But this is unlikely to be the last unpleasant surprise.

There is much tiresome overkill. Every night Chinese TV is showing relentless, huge, spectacular — and thus exhausting — performances celebrating the world's greatest Games before they even start. Yet it would be churlish not to wish the Chinese a successful Games. The first eight months of 2008 have been tough for the Chinese — from the winter freeze to the Tibet uprising, and from inflation worries to the Sichuan earthquake — and very far from the triumphal path that they wished for. They deserve this moment to be an uplifting one.

Moreover, there has been too much bitterness and disappointment, even in China's recent past. An old man deep in the countryside was filmed on TV, saying — close to tears — that he never thought he would see the day when the world would be coming to China, and that the Games would be held here. He must have lived through the Maoist years, when China was a closed world. It's not hard to imagine the sights he must have seen and the pain he must have lived through. There are hundreds of millions of such "ordinary" — yet each in his or her own way extraordinary — Chinese people, for whom the Games are a source of national pride.

It is only political elites that seem to want to twist them into something else. For China's citizens, something more affecting and simple is brought to the surface by what is happening: the feeling that this is their country, that they are happy to belong to it, and proud to see it take its respected and dignified place alongside every other.

There is more than enough room for the unexpected in China these days. As the clock counts down the last few days, I am startled by a taxi driver when the conversation turns — quite naturally, it seems — to corruption. I mention Chen Liangyu, the Shanghai Party Secretary who was placed under house arrest in September 2006 for allegedly diverting social security money into dodgy property deals. "I don't reckon Chen was a bad man," the driver said. "I don't care if he had 20 lovers, and spent his life carousing. But he did one thing right. Under him, Shanghai pulled itself forward. And he was the only one to think about how to cover pensions. In your country, you can retire and know you've got something. We've got nothing here. He knew the only way to make any money was to put all the city's funds into property. He was right. It's shot up in value. But of course, the central government hate this sort of independence. I say if we ever get a half-decent pension when we grow old, it'll be down to Chen, not those apes in Beijing." I think over what he said. "But where's the money he's said to have laundered?" "As far as I know, it's all still there. He hardly needs it now. He never touched a penny of it."

It seems symbolic to me. Three days before the young century's greatest public event, and this taxi driver — like almost everyone else you meet in Shanghai — seems both to have his mind on other things, and to see them for what they are, without illusion. The experience of this other great and modern Chinese city on Olympic eve leads me to a prediction: that during the Games, soon after the start — and as long as there isn't some sort of unplanned spectacle — the news will shift pretty quickly from all the politics to the usual rage and indignity of who wins and who loses (and who has taken drugs and who hasn't) in the sports events.

In short: finally, we got there. After the (hoped-for) relief of the opening, the Games will commence. In my view, and in that of most of the people I meet in China, that seems to be the right thing.

China Changes Itself: An Olympics Report

20 August 2008

The three-quarter point of the Olympic Games in Beijing passes with a host of sights and impressions already imprinted on the consciousness of both China and the world — from the beautified capital city and its friendly stage army of bright and enthusiastic volunteers, to the extraordinary performances of some of the world's great athletes and swimmers (as well as specialists in many more recondite sports). Even the crashing wave of Chinese emotion that accompanied the sudden pre-race departure of the local hero and 110-metres hurdles hope Liu Xiang — albeit followed, as night follows day, by some bitter denunciation of the athlete in China's febrile cyberspace — offers a vivid example of the kind of collective national sentiment that, increasingly, highlights global bonds as much as divisions.

The confounding — so far — of the more gloomy forecasts (smog, chaotic protests, internet censorship, terrorism — though watch Xinjiang) is a matter of profound relief to the authorities. It has even all been — so far — remarkably scandal-free (a few drug-test cases aside). Here, however, there is one big exception — the revelations over the artful manipulations of image and sound at Zhang Yimou's spectacular opening ceremony on 8 August 2008.

In some circumstances, the media's triple discovery — that the sweet nine-year-old girl Lin Miaoke chosen to perform the song that opened the Games had been miming to the nightingale voice of the (supposedly) less-charming seven-year-old Yang Peiyi, that the 29 giant firework "footprints" against the Beijing night sky had in fact been simulated for the TV audience, and that the costumed children representing China's notional 55 "ethnic minorities" were all Han Chinese — might have derailed the coverage of the entire event. Instead, and in the context of the subsequent (at the time of writing) 12 days of competition, the kerfuffle over the Bird's Nest stadium serves to highlight the fascinating non-sporting theme that is emerging from the Beijing Games: the sense that China's much-vaunted, championed, feared and discussed "transformation" is indeed becoming irreversible — and that its primary and perhaps most profound impact will be on China *itself*.

The miming mini-scandal in particular was the perfect moment of clashing values that, it could seem, many foreign journalists and media organisations had been waiting for. The inaugural ceremony had been almost too perfect; surely there must be some spots on the sun? When the proof of phoniness was found in the story of a small girl's uneven teeth, many members of the visiting media army were gleeful: now they had struck gold. A deeper look at the Zhang Yimou spectacular — aided by an awareness of the film director's transition from perceptive artist to stately heritage-peddler — goes some way to confirm the argument that China's control freakishness still crushes true individuality and spontaneity. True, there was a strong element of kitsch nationalism in this staged and triumphal pageant of historical and cultural achievement. China, apart from North Korea, is probably the only remaining country that can harness this degree of coordinating energy, focused resources and (since this is China) sheer multitudes for an event of this kind. The Pyongyang reference is telling: for all the technical wizardry, in part it evoked a more sinister world of mass rallies and conformist ultra-collectivism.

And yet, this was not *all* it was, and the fact that news of the ceremony's legerdemain moments have — so far — failed to define the "narrative" of the Beijing Olympics is also evidence of this. Indeed, a key to understanding what is happening in China as the Games approach their climax is the odd way that the opening spectacle conveyed power *and* vulnerability in the same moment.

In this combination — and the space between them — lurks something quite unexpected which I find myself surprised to admit: not just that the Beijing Olympics *will* change China, but that to some extent they already *have*. This is clearer if all the events and festivities are seen in the context of what went before, namely the consequences of winning the right to host (including extensive soul-searching about China's image in the world), the unsettling events of 2008 (the Tibet uprising, the Sichuan earthquake, the Torch relay protests) which have led to vehement criticism around the world of the country's political system and leadership.

China's leaders have been shocked and many of its people injured by this. They realise that it is not enough anymore to be known simply for economic success and dynamism; they feel they (and their country) deserve better. They are looking for a way forward and the concern with image revealed in the 8 August ceremony, as well as the top-down yet nervous treatment of foreign media at the Olympics — expose the fragility beneath the surface of China's new-found confidence.

China's leaders are thus in a difficult position as they look ahead from the Games to their next high-level annual Party Central Committee meetings in October 2008. How will they react? They can, in principle, take a hard line — China is right to do what it does, and react how it does; the rest of the world can think what it likes; the problem lies outside, not within. This, however, would be a return to the past that would jeopardise what China now needs, as well as being a guarantee of a longer war of attrition that — at its current stage of development — would be far from China's interests. China has never needed outside help more than now. It stands at the foot of a steep path that will be hard to climb. The Olympics reveal (and have helped guarantee) that it has many resources: the infrastructure, the capital and the will to carry itself forwards to becoming a modern, middle-income economy. It could even aspire to be much more than this. But it will need great assistance from the outside world, both in technology (to fix its severe environmental problems) and in internationalising its companies and brands.

If its leadership does realise the blindness of the first option and the necessity of the second, the immediate steps on China's upward path can begin. But this would mean also a continuation of perhaps the deepest change of all in the 2000s, one that the Olympics have both made clear and helped to further — that the Chinese people, complex and segmented and dispersed as they are, have and want a voice. Their demands for a bigger say in how their country is run are growing to the point where they will want far more than simply to entrust everything to the Communist Party and its inner divisions. The upward path that China's leadership has to take will face it with the need to start thinking about the greatest step of all — becoming a transparent, modern democracy.

The Olympics have already shown just how much China wants and needs to be part of the world. True, all the expense, the effort and the exposure has in part been the leadership's attempt to satisfy (and propitiate) Chinese citizens — including (and here the domestic and the global purposes fuse) by showing the people at home that their country matters in the world. This delicate predicament as much as the strength of the Chinese leadership came back to me while watching the pastiche version of the Chinese past at the Bird's Nest. The foundations of what China has become are far older than Mao Zedong or Sun Yat-sen. This extraordinary country — which embraces a fifth of humanity and thus which, by virtue of its very size, is global in almost all it does — is the work of the expansionist years in the middle of the Qing dynasty (1644–1911). Kangxi and Qianlong, the longest-lived and most influential of the 17th–18th-century emperors, are — by expanding imperial China's sphere of influence deep into inner Asia and beyond — the real architects of modern China. It is their ambitions which underlie the huge 21st-century challenge of trying to hold together this vast and contradictory entity together, and to make it a force for progress on its territory and in the world.

The combination of China's power and China's vulnerability that the Olympics have revealed make these Games a far more interesting moment than I had expected. The Olympics have been less a declaration of confidence than a loud demand to be noticed by a country that still has self-doubts. The leadership's assessment of the Beijing extravaganza will begin at the October 2008 meeting. It will be another pivotal political event. It is very probable that it will reflect how much those in charge will have learned from the last year, and that the outcome will be change in how China defines what it wants and aspires to be, and the way it communicates with the world.

The Olympics have already confirmed and reinforced to China's political elite the larger truth that the world now expects the country to be a truly important power. By October, if not before, it will come to realise that the Games were the easy part. A far bigger challenge will then begin — the creation of a modern political system to match and build on China's remarkable economic achievement of the last three decades.

China's Nervous Transition

22 September 2008

It is back to reality with a vengeance in China. The effects of a new era of global financial turmoil and a local scandal over tainted milk powder, have begun to consign the Beijing Olympics to history. A stream of political and economic challenges awaits the country's political leadership. Perhaps, most fundamentally, an extraordinary year of crisis and achievement enters its closing stages with fresh questions arising over the future of China's much-vaunted manufacturing model itself.

True, the late-summer events in China's capital city will not — as has so much else in China's modern history — be allowed to disappear down the memory hole. President Hu Jintao is not an expressive man, but even his ever-present enigmatic smile seemed to acquire a sincere glow at the closing ceremony of the Beijing Olympics on 24 August 2008. No wonder; China's expenditure of USD44 billion had its reward in the table-topping 51 gold medals China claimed. The sporting excitement of 16 days of competition, and that of the life-affirming Paralympic Games of 6–17 September which followed, made the problems of a difficult year — from Tibet to air pollution, social protest to corruption — seem distant (even if the unrest in Xinjiang, the most problematic of all China's restive regions, was felt even during the Games).

The Chinese people themselves seemed to rise to the occasion in appreciating the wonderful diversions of sport. But now, for government and citizens alike, it is back to reality — as the global financial troubles and the escalating milk powder scandal reveal all too plainly. Yet, even amidst these new economic and social tests, the members of China's Politburo will be obliged when they next meet to make an assessment of the whole Olympics exercise. They cannot fairly be denied a few moments of self-congratulation at the state's hosting of what was indeed an extraordinary event. Perhaps they will pause for a few moments too to mark the passing during the Games of the man in charge of China when the reform process started in 1978.

Hua Guofeng — the forgotten man of Chinese politics, even though he was Mao Zedong's personally chosen successor — died on 20 August 2008 at the age of 87. To his political rival Deng Xiaoping goes all the glory for what happened during the initial liberalisations in the 1980s, but Hua deserves credit for the quick challenge to the radical leadership of the "Gang of Four" and for helping to make the transition to the reformist era as smooth as eventually it was. It is easy now to forget how potentially unstable China was in those dark early years following the death of the "great helmsman". It didn't happen, but perhaps the Olympics should have stopped for just a minute to mark the passing of a man who was such a faithful servant of the Party.

In any case, the shape of the Party's and State's new hurdles are already becoming apparent now that the Games are over. The World Expo in Shanghai in 2010 — the next "big event" — will generate great excitement and pride, but it isn't quite in the league of the world's greatest sporting event. Many Chinese people already feel as if they've woken up with something of a hangover, which the milk powder controversy — which has claimed both lives and political casualties — will only intensify. Moreover, the economic woes consuming much of the world are blasting a chill wind onto the Chinese economic powerhouse. In these circumstances, the Politburo's room for quiet satisfaction will — insofar as it exists at all — be small.

This is where there is a problem, for which the Olympics with its wall-to-wall commercialism is a great, symbolic finale. James Kynge, the former *Financial Times* correspondent in Beijing and author of *China Shakes the World*,[4] outlined the leadership's predicament in stark terms in a fine recent analysis given at an academic conference in the UK. The rest of the world has for ten years been enjoying the benefits of China's export of deflation. China's exports, built on cheap labour and manufacturing costs, have brought the prices of consumer goods tumbling down. Much of the world cooks on barbecue grills that cost less than the price of meat prepared

---

[4] James Kynge, *China Shakes the World*, Orion Books, London, 2007.

on them. But, as James Kynge points out, there is a great pretence about all of this: for the prices of all the Chinese factors of production involved in the process — land, capital, labour costs and transport — have all been set by the state, and kept well below the proper market value.

Now, however, the free market is creeping into almost every area of China's economy, from utilities to employment. The result is a price correction in which markets set the rates. Local governments are thinking of new ways to sell or rent so-called state land in ways that can make them money; water is being sold in some areas of China, leading to sharp price increases; and labour shortages are beginning to be seen in a market that was until recently thought to offer a limitless supply of cheap workers. A new contract law introduced in January 2008 gives employees even greater rights and benefits.[5] For WalMart, Tesco and the like, this means the price of their exports is going to go up, and up again. In short, the era of "made in China" looks like it is drawing to a close. It will be a lengthy process; but suddenly, manufacturing in Vietnam or Cambodia, or even Laos, looks like it will become more straightforward and profitable than in China.

The Politburo may well look upon this as a mixed blessing. The manufacturing model they have adopted over the last three decades has ruined China's environment, and depleted most of its natural resources. It also increasingly fails to meet the needs of those who service it; the aspirations of hundreds of millions of Chinese migrant workers searching for employment in the cities are no longer satisfied by the prospect of manufacturing Barbie dolls for a few cents an hour. They have become more aware of their rights, more aware of what they want and less willing to forever be making sacrifices with no tangible return.

So the Politburo will only be able to give themselves a few moments to celebrate the "most successful Games ever". They will then need to move on to the more pressing business of where to direct the economy in the months and years ahead. Their foreign-investment strategy is at a critical juncture. Chinese banks are looking to spread themselves abroad more and more widely. For their part, there are signs that Coca-Cola and

---

[5]Han Dongfang, "Collective Bargaining and the New Labour Contract Law", *China Labour Bulletin*, 26 February 2008.

other multinationals now want to acquire — with full guarantees — assets and companies in China.

The 51 gold medals which China's sportsmen and sportswomen won was an amazing achievement; the impact of the Games on China's popular consciousness is less measurable, but much more significant. The Chinese leadership will need every particle of ingenuity and intelligence it has to manage the potential mess that could lay just a few steps ahead. Something it dreads is about to happen: it is starting to live in very interesting times, of which even the enormous convulsions on the world's financial markets are just one aspect. Hu Jintao and his colleagues may one day look back with nostalgia on the period when the only thing it had to worry about was the success of the Beijing Olympics. From here, they are in uncharted territory.

Gan Lulu and China: The Human Touch

12 July 2012

The great French philosopher Roland Barthes once wrote that fashion was a world created by the gaze of men.[6] The same might be said of China's public landscape, dominated as it is by men (usually in their late 40s and above) from a rather homogenous educational and cultural background. This is even more true of the power elite: the Chinese Communist Party's membership is 80% male, and there are only a handful of women on the Central Committee (and none on the Politburo Standing Committee). The gaze of men creates the world of China.

Against this background, it may seem strange to propose that a 27-year-old Shandong model called Gan Lulu, famous for a brief but sensational appearance in a tight black dress ("more flesh than fabric" said one observer) at the Beijing motor fair in April 2012, is a significant figure in modern China. But in many ways, she is — more perhaps than many inside as well as outside China realise.

Gan Lulu, who in time-honoured fashion graduated from one of Beijing's many acting academies, is armed with a ferociously pushy mother who shares the spotlight at her public appearances, snapping photos beside the

---

[6]Roland Barthes, *The Fashion System*, University of California Press, Berkeley, 1967.

Chinese paparazzi. The mother's interventionist role in the daughter's career includes posting a film of Gan Lulu on the internet in which she berates her for not having a boyfriend and preparing to marry and settle down. The somewhat contradictory moral economy of "selling" your daughter while trying to promote traditional norms is routine for modern China, where the combination of rapid growth and social change has produced an era of rich confusion.

But for all the confusion — and for all the snobbish disdain people like Gan attract — Gan Lulu does represent something important. She, or the phenomenon she embodies, may even come to exert a more enduring influence than the interminable leadership transition still grinding forward in Beijing. That process is being conducted in an environment dense with scrutiny and inference yet devoid of information, in which even a stray comment about the weather by a Politburo member is an occasion for quasi-mystical runes-reading (witness He Guoqiang who, on a visit to the megacity of Chongqing after the fall of its big boss Bo Xilai, unfavourably contrasted the climate there with Beijing's — which was instantly viewed as a signal of Bo's imminent political decapitation in the capital).

After 1949 in China, it was a cultural given that politics was everywhere. It invaded your private space, your intimate relations, your working life, your travels and your language. The apogee of this pervasive influence was the "great Cultural Revolution" (1966–1976), when everyday events were choreographed according to a political programme formulated around the "great helmsman", Mao Zedong. His image was on every wall, his myth saturated the country's artistic life, his edicts were ubiquitous, and his persona was invested with superhuman abilities.

These days, the interface between politics and daily life in China is more subtle. Yet it is remains, and for the average Chinese to attempt what people in the West would take for granted — "depoliticising" one's life, adopting a stance of nonchalance or complete indifference to leaders' claim on their attention — still proves surprisingly difficult. Politics might no longer be so much "in control" (as a favourite ultra-Maoist slogan had it) but it continues to supply a noisy, inescapable mood music as the backdrop to most Chinese people's lives.

After all, they will be obliged to deal with officials at key points in their careers, especially if they become successful. They will need to be careful what they write on the internet, how they interact in society and with whom, what news they read and what cultural choices they make. In all of these areas, politics somehow gets factored in. Even a trenchant and high-profile critic of the Beijing government like Ai Weiwei spends much time denying that he is making "political" statements — only for this to become part of a political domain he seeks to avoid.

It is said that in China a person can curse the government as long as it is done discreetly, without either committing it to print or taking any resulting action. Well, China's rulers may be able to tolerate most cursing; but the one thing China can't put up with is a bold, cool refusal to allow them and their political messages to have any purchase, moral reach or cultural impact on the Chinese citizen's life. For Beijing's elite, as for Oscar Wilde, the one thing worse than being talked about is not being talked about.

Many Chinese, living with this reality, adopt a kind of self-aware cynicism. This strategy leads them to respond to the dance of interest, greed and hypocrisy at the summit of China's system, or to the maze of allegations surrounding Bo Xilai and his immediate family, by turning away with a weary sigh and wishing a plague on it all. But cynicism, again recalling Wilde, is a cheap and shallow option. China deserves better.

Which brings us back to Gan Lulu. Again, it would seem foolhardy to pile political meaning onto a self-promoting young model whose weapons are an assertive mum, a wardrobe of skimpy clothes and an ability to draw the puritanical ire of many thousands of China's Weibo followers.

Yet, in the distorting conditions of today's China, where the government's relentless attention seeking is matched by the visceral hostility of anti-government activists and the alienation of many of their faithful followers, Gan's triumphantly apolitical appeal — straighter, more honest and (yes) more innocent — gives her a rare integrity.

Gan could not possibly be recruited by a Chinese political class that, whatever bedlam is going on in its members' private lives, is outwardly super-priggish. And if she were tempted, she would soon be buried under the sort of elite pomposity that comes as easily as breathing to so many of China's privileged.

By the standards of those around her, Gan Lulu seems far more a pointer to China's future. In her style of expression, the way she chooses to exercise influence and power, and her curiously moving reach beyond herself and her world, she is a symbol of what China is becoming. The Chinese Communist Party, if it were wise, could learn one important lesson from her: that the future of China is not just about politics or as was said by Bill Clinton during the US presidential election campaign in 1992 "the economy, stupid" — it's also about humanity.

Chapter Three

China and the Outside World

From 2007 to 2013, there was a puzzling disconnect. Outside of China, it seemed that wherever one went, whether in Europe, the US or Australia, China loomed like a mighty space ship about to cast its shadow across the land, a bit like the invading army from another planet in Richard Ford's Independence Day *— unified, disciplined, rich and confident. Business people, officials and analysts often spoke of some imminent onslaught of Chinese money, Chinese influence and Chinese trade. The statistics that issued over this period were impressive — largest foreign investor, largest exporter, second-largest importer, second-largest economy... It all seemed to presage an historic transition between an exhausted, stretched United States riven by internal divisions within its polity and bound to the trillions it had poured into Iraq and Afghanistan. Were we witnessing the rise of a new super power, aiming for global dominance?*

That narrative dissipated almost the moment one cleared customs at Beijing airport. Any interaction with officials, diplomats or Chinese people, made for a much more ambiguous story — the same ambiguity displayed in China's own internal governance and politics referred to in the last chapter. For most officials, the idea of being pushed into a position as G2 next to the US was deeply unwelcome. For them, there were legions of challenges in the country around them — inequality between and within different provinces, environmental nightmares, huge issues about keeping an increasingly vociferous and expectant population content. Why get mixed up in the issues of countries beyond China's borders, unless there were tangible and specific things connected to national interest?

Despite the fact that many in the Chinese government acted and spoke like they would have been more than happy to revert to a position of splendid isolation a little akin to the US before the First World War a century beforehand, there was also pragmatic acknowledgement that with so many energy and investment interests abroad now, this was not a feasible position to take. Like it or not, the uprisings in the Middle East — in particular those in Egypt, Libya and Syria — and the attempts by Iran to nuclearise itself were issues that China had to take a position on. There were no easy diplomatic answers for China here, as the pieces in this chapter show, with the situation in Egypt in almost constant disarray since 2011 and the conflict in Syria, according to British Foreign Secretary William Hague in 2013, decades from resolution. China's increased determination to stop US-led involvement in these areas has been a striking aspect of the early 2010s.

Things were no less easy elsewhere. A puzzling moment of assertiveness by China in 2009, during the first visit of newly elected US President Barack Obama was rewarded with concerted US and international pushback. Things were most difficult, however, over the maritime border disputes with neighbours of China that it shared the most contentious and complex relations with — Japan and Vietnam in particular. Throughout 2010 and onto 2013, arguments piled up with each of these about the status of specific contested islands, and the best way to sort out rights to exploitation of natural resources while leaving the almost insoluble issue of final sovereignty alone. To crown all of this, China had to face a US whose leaders were rebalancing their forces and their interests to Asia, and who acted, at least to many commentators and officials in Beijing, just like they were trying to contain the country and thwart its interests.

It is no surprise that this section contains discussions of North Korea. If there was one issue that placed China between a rock and a hard place, then the handling of their impoverished, failing neighbour was it. From 2007, North Korea (the Democratic People's Republic of Korea; DPRK) delivered a series of unpleasant shocks, not the least the sudden death of its dear leader Kim Jong-il after several visits to China over a short period of time in 2010 and 2011. Kim's demise, however, did not lead to any easing up of challenging issues, with 2013 marked by a crescendo of noisy threatening behaviour under the juvenile leadership of the new leader, Kim Jong-un. The North Korean case illustrated one puzzling anomaly; that a country like China, lauded as increasingly powerful and influential internationally was unable to reign in such a seemingly reliant client state on its borders, despite the fact this state was crossing one of the major red lines of acquiring nuclear weapons directly against China's interests. It seemed therefore that it was not just a challenge for those outside of China to work out what sort of power it really was. There were many within the country, some in very senior positions, who were just as mystified. "The problem is," an academic from Shanghai said to me in 2012, "you all want us to say who we are, and what we stand for, and what we want, and yet we haven't had the time to decide that for ourselves. We simply don't know."

Chimerica: Obama Visits Beijing

27 October 2009

Any visit by a US President to the People's Republic of China is a big event. This is certainly true of Barack Obama's forthcoming trip, part of a week-long, four-nation tour (also including Japan, Singapore and South Korea) on 12–19 November 2009 and his first overseas trip since being awarded the Nobel Peace Prize.

China is preparing hard for its latest presidential visitor. Whatever under-lying tensions and policy differences there might be, a constant feature of Chinese diplomatic behaviour is that when faced with the big guys in their midst its elite knows how to deploy the extravagant host's skills of ceremony and flattery. Bill Clinton irritated China greatly during his presidency, and insisted on speaking about human rights when he visited in 1998 (the first post-Tiananmen trip); none of this prevented him from being lavishly received. George W. Bush's arrival in Beijing for the first of his two 2002 visits was eerie; I recall having to take massive detours in order to drive a short distance home, so many and huge were the roadblocks erected to protect the world's most powerful man.

Barack Obama will be guaranteed equal levels of security, even though he will be far safer in China than he is at home. After all, he receives four times the number of death threats than Bush did — and that's only the ones we know about. If he is history's most protected man it is for good reason. The ferocity of the bile and spleen directed against him by sections of the US right is dizzying.

But in China, the purpose of the huge security cordon around him will be more a ritual of honour and admiration than a fearful response to any threat. The Chinese might not know much about him, but it is clear they are both intrigued and impressed by the first African-American President. Moreover, the relationship between Obama and his counterpart Hu Jintao has started more positively than any such among their predecessors; the contrast is notably sharp with the more direct and tactile Jiang Zemin, who for all his famous chemistry with leaders like Clinton and Bush (and French President Jacques Chirac) became embroiled in numerous spats and ended up achieving little.

The stiff, even somewhat robotic President Hu (a man widely seen as the world's second most powerful man) seems to be enjoying something close to a warm relationship with Obama. At London's G20 summit on 2 April 2009 they were reported to have got on well. Perhaps the key lies in a shared element in their background. Those who have met Hu often say that he comes across more like an academic than the leader of the world's most ruthless political machine, and Obama too is a cerebral, scholarly kind of politician. Whether the bond will lead to measurable political progress, however, remains to be seen.

The current harmony between Beijing and Washington is a striking departure from the days when every issue became a dispute shadowed by the ominous language of "containment". Now, the EU has replaced the US as China's target: a hectoring, uncooperative and multilayered interlocutor that constantly reproaches it on subjects it doesn't want to hear about. The bitter feelings towards the EU have grown since 2007, in part out of the Union's refusal — heavily influenced by Angela Merkel and Nicolas Sarkozy, its two most powerful national figures — to grant China market economy status. The criticisms of China's policy over Tibet have also played a part. China has despite this become the EU's largest trade partner; but the sour mood makes the EU–China summit in Nanjing on 30 November 2009 an important event where some of this damage could be on view.

The contrast in sentiment became clearer to me in Beijing in August 2009, when a Chinese university teacher turned from expressing a barely disguised disgust over the EU's "tone of moral superiority" towards China to declaring that the US had "got China right and approached issues with the proper manner". The pattern was echoed a few weeks later at a meeting in London, when a very senior Chinese leader warned that "the EU needs to be less complacent and arrogant" while praising the US as "always so flexible" and predicting that it will "continue to be the world's only superpower".

After years of hearing the US denounced in China for its disrespectful tone, all this comes as a surprise. In its way it is another tribute to Barack Obama's political and communications skills (albeit the US President has been on the receiving end of severe criticism about his lack of actual achievement so far); even more so in the sense that the US President's approach has done more than won a certain respect from the Chinese — it has also unsettled them, and at all levels.

How has this happened? Obama's instinct to reach out and attempt to work with China — in a variety of areas, from climate change to energy, global security to the international economy — may be a necessity from Washington's perspective; but it has also had the effect of creating divisions among the Chinese political and economic elite.

For some members of this elite, the forcing of China (even by the use of "soft power") into a position where it becomes in effect a co-superpower is no more than an elaborate trick that preys on China's vulnerabilities; the process will end, they argue, by destabilising and weakening the country. For example, if China is dragged into accepting international commitments far beyond its borders — and in areas beyond its understanding or interest — the result will be to divide the country. Instead, China must continue to work on building up its own capacity and strengthening itself.

For others, the main point of concern is timing. Even if the US is sincere in seeing China as a partner, almost an equal one, this whole process is happening too quickly. The homeland, they argue, is having to run hard merely to cope with myriad internal problems, and cannot prematurely become a world power or operate abroad without serious risks.

Among both sides, there is a clear and honest admission that China is simply not ready for the role that Barack Obama's administration appears to want to assign to it. The increasing demands for China to get involved, even when met by a well-intentioned response, are starting to worry Chinese policy-makers. They are the ones who know best just how immense are the political, economic and social challenges facing China in the coming decade.

Behind this division is a shared reluctance to assume too many or too onerous "global" responsibilities, a reality very different from the routine picture of China as a confident and voracious rising power. The implication is that it is Washington that will have to continue to set the pace in most critical foreign-policy regions; where Afghanistan, Iran and the Israeli–Palestinian conflict are concerned, China will continue to concede US leadership and seek to avoid entanglement.

There is one crucial area, however, that China can't avoid: the international community's dealings with North Korea (the Democratic People's Republic of Korea; DPRK). Here Obama can, and should, press China to do more. Kim Jong-il's mercurial regime is in one of its less provocative phases, but a return to its usual mix of escalating rhetoric and missile-tests is almost certain. China has influence in North Korea, whether or not it accepts this, and it could do more to persuade the Pyongyang regime — politically, economically and diplomatically — to negotiate, and to move towards constructive agreement on real goals.

The most important of these must be an immediate cessation of its nuclear programme. North Korea's nuclear capacity at present is still weak, and China has an opportunity to take a leading role by using the leverage of its aid, economic-cooperation and energy-supply links with the country to achieve a historic shift in North Korea's stance.

The window could close, and in a way that would change all calculations. If in future North Korea launched a direct missile at Japan, or even South Korea, the warm atmospherics and kind words between the US and China at the moment would mean nothing. Better that Barack Obama and Hu Jintao anticipate and avert disaster than find they are woken in the middle of the night with the news that this time, something bad has happened. There is a time and a place for bold leadership as well as proper caution, and Beijing in November 2009 is one of those.

North Korea's Fate, Chimerica's Test

With Jiyoung Song

7 December 2009

The relatively smooth passage of Barack Obama's first visit to east Asia from 12–19 November 2009 — where he visited Japan, Singapore (for the Asia Pacific Economic Cooperation Summit), China and South Korea — reflected a notable aspect of the first year of this US presidency: that it has been largely free, concerns with China over trade and Japan over the location of military bases apart, from the kind of tensions with the region that marked the early periods of the Bill Clinton and George W. Bush presidencies.

Yet the oddly muted welcome to Obama, and the mini-buffeting given to him by the media at home over his alleged kowtowing to the Chinese and an excessively low bow to Japan's emperor, have tended to deflect attention from a vital and unresolved regional issue which blocks a clear path to resolution: namely, policy towards North Korea (the Democratic People's Republic of Korea; DPRK).

The possession and test firing of nuclear weapons by North Korea is a central part of this question, but — as indicated by the latest news of dangerous food insecurity and discontent over a substantial currency revaluation — it is far from being the only aspect. Moreover, the future of North Korea is an area where active cooperation between Beijing and Washington is as essential to progress as in the vital area of climate change.

The lack of an open discussion between the US and the People's Republic of China over what to do about North Korea is in this respect an exception to their wide-ranging exchanges over other questions of shared interest (among them climate change, financial matters, Iran and Afghanistan).

China has a somewhat ambiguous stock response when its attitude towards the Pyongyang regime is raised: namely, that it has close historical and political ties to its neighbour yet at the same time limited influence over it. Thus — even though it may complain about the "dear leader" Kim Jong-il's manipulative behaviour and is evidently irritated by North Korea's constant desire to talk directly to the US — China can never break with its "little brother". The visit of China's Defence Minister Liang Guanglie to Pyongyang on 22 November 2009 — marked by familiar rhetoric of unbending solidarity — fits this pattern well.

True, China can justify its policy stance in broader strategic terms. In chairing the six-party talks over North Korea since 2003 (involving Russia, Japan and the US as well as China and the two Koreas), Beijing has exercised some responsibility in trying to persuade North Korea to observe international norms. This made Pyongyang's nuclear tests of 2006 and 2009 a particular rebuff to China's patient diplomacy.

But China does have more influence in North Korea than it cares to acknowledge. It is North Korea's main aid donor (providing almost 50% of the total), is the source of 90% of the country's energy resources and — underlying tensions notwithstanding — has more access and space to press its views upon the elite in Pyongyang than does any other country. In addition, China's ability to face down the US and the EU diplomatically when it feels certain of its ground is well attested; there is no reason in principle why it cannot use its resources to advance a diplomatic solution in its own "backyard".

At the heart of the problem are North Korea's nuclear ambitions. China and the US both see a nuclear (or gradually nuclearising) North Korea as inherently destabilising, not least because it serves as an excuse for other countries in Asia to justify their own arms building. In formal terms, the denuclearisation of North Korea and stability in north-east Asia represents a shared agenda between Beijing and Washington, leading both to press North Korea to engage in positive negotiations within the six-party framework.

But China's approach to North Korea and its future is also caught between contradictory interests and objectives. For however much the Beijing leadership would prefer a non-nuclear North Korea, it would also be deeply worried by the prospect of a disarmed North Korea — perhaps followed by a unified state on the peninsula, backed by the US, and committed to (and even promoting) democracy and human rights. Could the Chinese leadership accept, for example, a "peaceful" US military presence just across the Yalu River after Korean unification?

This internal dilemma helps explain the absence of progress on North Korea between Hu Jintao and Barack Obama in Beijing. Yet this is an area where President Obama could (and arguably needs to) earn his Nobel accolade. For a trustworthy partnership with China is the key to North Korea's denuclearisation and disarmament. To achieve it, Obama needs a clear assessment of China's willingness to persuade the "little brother" to abandon its military-first politics and develop the country economically and politically; and more broadly for the US and China to understand each other's objectives over North Korea as clearly as possible.

The reform of North Korea's governmental system — not "merely" its denuclearisation and guarantees of non-proliferation — is a major concern across the region: most immediately of all for South Korea. Thus, a nuclear-free North Korea, however hard it will be to get there, is not the end of the story. Many other major problems will have to be addressed in managing the country's transition to a more sustainable society, among them malnutrition, gender equality, an ingrained militarism and a potential mass exodus.

This in turn raises a crucial question for all the actors involved about the medium-term future: whether the two Koreas and the region's interests would be best served by two (peaceful, disarmed, cooperative) Korean states, or by a single (unified and powerful) one. All the leadership skills of Barack Obama and Hu Jintao and their associates in particular will be called upon to resolve this issue; as much as climate change, it's a subject that requires frank dialogue, sustained commitment and clear objectives. If that was missing in the US President's first tour of the region, it cannot be long postponed.

China and America: The Uses of Vulnerability

8 June 2010

A number of events in April–June 2010 have seemed to suggest that relations between the US and China are back on track after a difficult period. They include Hu Jintao's visit to Washington in May for the opening of the international review-conference on the nuclear non-proliferation treaty, the suspension of arguments about the need to revalue the Chinese currency and discussions on the latest crisis over North Korea.

The world's two most important powers have, it seems, moved beyond a period of difficult, sometimes fraught, exchanges. There is still potential for disputes, such as over Taiwan or climate change, but overall the picture is one of a return to business as normal. However, the few months of edginess from late 2009 were significant, and examining it may reveal something of the tension that often underlies the vital relationship between the People's Republic of China and the US.

It is not an over exaggeration to say that for four decades the overriding priority of Chinese foreign policy has been to stick close to Washington. In the dark days of the Cultural Revolution of the late 1960s, Mao Zedong instructed some old comrades to advise him on how to reconnect with the US. Within three years, Richard Nixon had made his historic visit, and the relationship was set on the path it has followed ever since. Deng Xiaoping consolidated it further by crafting a whole policy around getting benefits, including investment, from increased links with the world's most powerful economy. This was condensed into an edict: "keep a low profile, build up our capacity and be cooperative". It could be argued from the perspective of 2010 that it is the most successful piece of foreign-policy wisdom in China's modern history.

The strength of the relationship at elite level was seen after June 1989, when President George H. W. Bush helped China to rejoin the international community quicker than many expected as it faced relative isolation in the wake of the Tiananmen Square massacre. From its side, Beijing refused to allow periodic clashes — over Taiwan, joining the World Trade Organization, or US interventions in Yugoslavia (where the Chinese embassy was bombed) or Iraq — to deflect it from Mao's strategy of sticking close to the US.

Beijing has its foreign-policy disputes and factions, however, even if they are not always as public as Washington's. And in the background of the arguments between the two capitals, a deeper internal battle over China's foreign-policy soul can sometimes be glimpsed. The useful if familiar distinction between hawks and doves is one entry-point that can help make sense of it.

The hawks (who are also often both nationalists and leftists) believe that it is no longer necessary to stay faithful to Deng Xiaoping's edict. They see a US that is in decline, yet continuing to pursue brutally self-interested objectives; the attempt to bind China into climate-change commitments that will restrict its economic growth, and to entice the country into expensive military programmes which will squander its hard-worn reserves and lead it along the same path to oblivion as the Soviet Union.

The conclusion is that China must now prepare to live in a world where battles — over energy resources, Taiwan and China's territorial integrity — will soon make sticking close to the US redundant and self-defeating. The argument here is reflected in the calls made at the National People's Congress in March 2010 that China needs to have aircraft carriers, and to move from being a land power to becoming a naval one.

The doves see a China where the country's USD2.6 trillion reserves co-exist with a *per capita* GDP that ranks 115 in the world (behind, for example, Namibia), and note that China's water resources are 50% more polluted than had been reported even a year before. They highlight the fact that 12 million petitions are delivered each year to the central government, evidence both of a society in ferment and a state that has failed to build a credible legal order. To take on the US now would be catastrophic; indeed, the day of encounter recedes into the distance. In this view, the most China realistically can hope to be is a perpetual number two.

The hawkish-nationalist case has a strong appeal to the Chinese public's heartstrings, not least in its focusing on a sense of historic grievance. Wang Xiaodong, a vehement exponent of this view, talks of China as at last fulfilling its aspiration to proper hard power, and jettisoning the soft-power strategy pursued before the Beijing Olympics in 2008. All that ever led to, he argues, was grief. "We [should] answer our critics with force, because that is all they have ever given to us," he says, bemoaning that fact that even China's heralded economic system has been built on the "blood and sweat of Chinese cheap labour to make the Western consumers rich".[1]

But there is a big problem in adopting a more hardline course. Wang Hui, among the most respected leftists, says, "the US comes to our borders, and sometimes is *inside* our borders".[2] America remains a country with 680 military installations in 120 countries, a USD780-billion defence budget and technical capacity decades ahead of anyone else. Even the Chinese military's strategy of focusing on non-conventional capacity building in "information systems" has been hit in the confrontations with Google. The nationalists see the latter as an inevitable warning shot from the US: go back into your boxes once more.

A report published in March 2010 vividly illustrates why the doves are so concerned.[3] In 2008–2009, China's military spending increased by 14% to USD80 billion. A much less noticed figure is the USD85-billion budget for internal security. China spends more on policing itself than it does on protecting itself from the outside world. This gives tangible insight into the vulnerabilities of the internal situation. The doves know well that if China had not achieved 9% growth in 2009, if it had shrunk like several major

---

[1] Paul Eckhert, 'Special Report: Cables show U.S. sizing up China's next leader', *Reuters*, 17 February 2011. Available online at http://www.reuters.com/article/2011/02/17/us-wiki-china-xi-idUSTRE71G5WH20110217. Accessed 9 October 2013.

[2] Wang Hui, *The End of the Revolution: China and the Limits of Modernity*, Verso, London, 2011.

[3] Stockholm International Peace Research Institute, *Recent Trends in Military Expenditure*. Available online at www.sipri.org/research/armaments/milex/recent-trends.

Western economies, the regime would have been hit by enormous unrest. Chinese politics exist on an economic cliff edge.

Both doves and (probably) hawks know that from 2012 to 2020 the Chinese Communist Party will have to face acute challenges. Among the most acute will be establishing a proper legal system where courts might one day hold the Party to account against its will; a proper legal basis for civil society to prevent social explosion; and a system of accountability that can address the issue of corruption. China towards 2020 will be a society where two people of working age will be supporting one who is retired, and where the gender imbalance resulting from the one-child policy will produce a surplus of 50 million single men. There is peril here for the Chinese Communist Party leadership at every step of the way.

Indeed, so great are the tasks ahead that the 2007–2010 period — the very time when much of the rest of the world suffered during the economic downturn — may even come to be viewed by the top Party bosses as being a kind of golden age. But there is no escape from emerging problems, and there are no easy options in confronting them. And a Chinese elite divided among itself is a recipe for more disagreement, attrition and volatility in relation to the outside world.

The Chinese leadership's awareness of the vulnerabilities of its position is reflected in Premier Wen Jiabao's comment made directly to President Obama in November 2009: "We do not want to be in a G2. We are not ready. We have too many of our own problems". The US and other Western countries should show a similar realism, that is, by supporting the Beijing doves as China approaches a painful (and perhaps imminent) political transition, while being clear about their own national interests. If the West gets it right, China may yet emerge on the other side as a modernised country and a more stable and more amenable partner, rather than the aggressive nationalist behemoth much of the world fears and some influential voices in China are tempted by.

China and Tony Blair: The Wealth Circuit

15 September 2010

The Shanghai summer of 2010 was so hot and steaming that even Shanghainese complained about it. But close behind as conversation topic for many in the city, at least when confronted with a visitor from the UK, is the lucrative exploits of Britain's former Prime Minister, Tony Blair.

During his premiership (1997–2007), Blair visited the People's Republic of China only twice. Now, he passes through Beijing and Shanghai every few months. There is no evidence that his current projects — including the promotion of his modestly titled book *A Journey*[4] — extend to any public role in the area: brokering a peace initiative, promoting the green economy, even preaching the merits of globalisation. The conclusion must be that he is here to chase his new passion — making money.

Many British people are sharply critical of their former leader's embrace of a super-rich lifestyle fuelled by enormous payments for "consultancy" speeches and personal appearances. Chinese people, by contrast, tend to discuss his presence in their midst with the steady tolerance towards personal accumulation of wealth that is one of their most striking characteristics. In part this reflects an internalisation of the message Deng Xiaoping is reputed to have given at the start of the epic reform process he initiated in 1978, "to get rich is glorious".

The heartland of the reforms was the southern settlement of Shenzhen, near the border with Hong Kong. Shenzhen was a small Cantonese fishing town, which — along with three others — was nominated in 1980 as a special economic zone (SEZ). The strong debate among the Party elite about giving the SEZ permission to manufacture and export for foreign enterprises was resolved within two years, when Shenzhen was posting growth rates of 45%. Even hardliners of the time like Deng Liqun fell silent before shock-and-awe growth like this.

Shenzhen is now a city of 10 million people, with *per capita* GDP levels close to the most developed countries and a middle-class containing some of the China's most dynamic — and internationalised — entrepreneurs. It may now be playing a different role in China's future, as a place of sporadic political experimentation. The city has a poor cultural image (its best offering so far is a replica of major global attractions displayed in a public park) — but it is right next to Hong Kong, with its openness and (albeit limited) democratic institutions.

---

[4]Tony Blair, *A Journey*, Arrow, London, 2011.

Shenzhen organised its own township elections in the late 1990s, although these failed to develop further. But China's Premier Wen Jiabao and President Hu Jintao have during recent visits both referred (in different terms) to the need for deeper political reform. The idea has started to circulate that Shenzhen may become a special political zone as well as an economic one. Where Shenzhen and Tony Blair intersect is that it is only places like this and the nearby Dongguan that can afford his now astronomical speaking fees. Blair was reported in 2007 to have earned USD500,000 for one short speech in the city. Now the Cantonese are among the world's shrewdest business people, and some journalists inquired whether his hosts in the area might feel short-changed. On the contrary, Blair's mere presence for a time in their city was seen as money well spent. Blair's ability to talk Cantonese people out of such sums impressed almost everyone I spoke to in China about this — including the Cantonese themselves.

The Chinese also recognise that Blair's visits are closely tied to China's rise towards the status of a global superpower. Among the many other consequences and problems this brings is that China will join the US and other countries as part of a lucrative "global circuit" of eminent former leaders. The shifting balance of world financial power may even make China a more attractive destination as corporate and institutional income streams start to flow more thickly. And the appeal of China to leaders such as Tony Blair will not be lessened by the fact that most of his audiences will understand very little of what they are saying.

A broader generational shift is also occurring. Political leaders are getting younger (Blair was 43 when he reached the top job, Barack Obama 47); this means too that ex-leaders are ever younger — and hang around longer (Obama, if re-elected, will be 55 when he leaves office — which could mean 30 more years of public activity of some sort). Bill Clinton is already setting the standard.

By the time the "sixth generation" of Chinese leaders comes to power after 2022, will China become an active source for speakers as well as a staging post on this lecture circuit? China's senior leaders are now obliged to retire at 68. Hu Jintao, Wen Jiabao and their successors may still be active for a decade or more after they retire. After the leadership transition in 2012, will they begin to speak at conferences in Europe and North America for massive fees? Will they even produce lengthy "revealing memoirs" on the

Tony Blair model, containing lurid detail of mutual loathing on the Politburo tempered by pious claims that they had to maintain face for the sake of a "harmonious society"?

There is, it is remarkable to note, a precedent here in the memoir of ex-Politburo member Li Lanqing, released in 2009 — though admittedly these restricted themselves to a fraction of his career, with no mention of the events in Tiananmen in 1989.[5] And one political victim of that tragedy, Party Secretary Zhao Ziyang, secretly wrote and — in the West — published his reflections on the debates among the leadership before and during the crisis.

Perhaps in turn the West has something to learn. In the 1980s, a group of China's elder leaders was gathered into an informal advisory council. Something of the sort exists in the transnational group known as "The Elders". A model that encourages a focused contribution to the public good from former politicians rather than individual enrichment would be at least worth aiming for. And even China's fiercest critics would not wish on it a local version of Tony Blair, a statesman-turned-salesman with himself and the faded aura of power the extortionate product.

China and the Egyptian Uprising

With Cassidy Hazelbaker

2 March 2011

The phenomenon of massive demonstrations uniting a huge public around the aspiration to change a country's leadership and renovate the governing system is at the centre of the remarkable uprisings in much of the Arab world in the first months of 2011. The successful overthrow of presidents in Tunisia and Egypt are their early fruits, but the process of democratic change is clearly unfinished and has at least the potential to go far wider.

Even a cursory knowledge of modern Chinese history suggests that the gathering of thousands of students in Tiananmen Square in the centre of Beijing in May–June 1989 has some parallels with the Arab revolts.

---

[5]Li Lanqing, *Breaking Through: The Birth of China's Opening-Up Policy*, Oxford University Press, Oxford, 2010.

There are also many differences, not least that the Tiananmen movement was eventually crushed by state violence (though the armed assault on sleeping protesters in Bahrain, the shooting of others in Yemen and the strife in Libya might seem at first sight to offer parallels with the brutal treatment of Chinese students in 1989).

What makes the possible linkage between China and Egypt (the biggest and most momentous of the Middle East events) more intriguing is that the information-control operatives of the Chinese Communist Party seem to be encouraging it even as they attempt to dismiss it out of hand. The Egyptian protests began on 25 January 2011. From that moment, news and searches about Egypt and its then President Hosni Mubarak on the Chinese internet were severely restricted (as they had been in regard to the Tunisian turmoil that was sparked on 17 December 2010).

What information there has been about the historic events in Cairo, Alexandria and other Arab cities (and most recently in Libya) is largely confined to the evacuation of Chinese tourists or workers. The protests and their causes — dire living conditions, frustration at unemployment, and anger at corrupt and repressive governments — have been ignored or skated over in official media.

This Chinese reaction raises the closely linked questions of whether any comparison can be made between the Arab mobilisations (in particular those in Egypt) and the situation in China, and why the Chinese government appears so fearful of a possible "contagion". China and Egypt, at least on the surface, share a number of characteristics. Each has been long ruled by an autocratic system, far from anything near a functioning democracy; each is marked by extreme inequality, with a core of very wealthy people surrounded by widespread poverty; each society has a major problem of corruption; and each depends on rapid economic growth to provide jobs and contain discontent.

But the differences are equally stark. China's economy has rapidly expanded over the three decades of "reform", with GDP growth averaging around 10% per year even during the West's major post-2007–2008 financial crisis. Egypt's economy has also grown substantially in the 2000s, although its peak of 5% annual growth is not enough to keep pace with a rising population and its accompanying needs — even the official unemployment rate is around 10%, and affects many university graduates.

China is the world's second-largest economy, the world's largest exporter, and has received USD570 billion in foreign direct investment (FDI). Egypt is the 27th-largest (with an economy of USD500 billion, roughly equal to Slovenia and Azerbaijan), and receives USD70 billion in FDI. There are also overlaps and contrasts in the nature of protest and opposition in both countries. Egypt's movement of 2011 directed its energies at one very specific objective — the removal of Hosni Mubarak from power. In 1989, the students assembling in Tiananmen Square pointed their fingers less at the then paramount leader Deng Xiaoping than at a system which (they said) fostered corruption.

Egypt's former ruling party, the National Democratic Party, has tolerated the existence of opposition parties (though surrounding them with restrictions and harassment); in China, any impulse to formalise opposition is ruthlessly crushed. True, social protests in China are common — around 90,000 incidents a year according to one estimate which reflects a high level of social discontent. Yet the Chinese Communist Party maintains a tight grip on its citizens to prevent any manifestation of the kind of massive, organised unrest that felled Mubarak.

The degree of dissimilarity between the two systems and societies notwithstanding, Beijing is evidently nervous about the possibility that the Arab democratic virus will infect China. This anxiety is part of a consistent pattern. The "colour revolutions" that swept through several states of the former Soviet bloc (Georgia, Ukraine, Kyrgyzstan) in the early to mid-2000s made Beijing think hard about whether China could be vulnerable to a similar process, with state-controlled think tanks being commissioned to report on why the popular insurgencies had occurred and how they could be avoided.

The most worrying element of the Egyptian events for Beijing is their combination of speed and unexpectedness. An unforeseen upsurge of mass protest led in only 18 days to the ousting (and rapid discrediting) of a commanding president who had ruled for 30 years. More widely, even in early December 2010, no one predicted that exactly two months later, peaceful popular action would drive from power two of the Arab world's longest-serving leaders.

The Chinese Communist Party knows that a series of small incidents can soon escalate. After all, it is this very Party that made famous the slogan, "a single spark can start a prairie fire". The lesson it draws is that the key to retaining power is eternal vigilance. In practice, now, that means two things. First, the Party will be taking a rigorous look at whether the Egyptian scenario — especially the space given there for individual voices to cry out, merge, gather, organise and make demands — is conceivable in China, and how it can be averted. Second, the Party will be scrutinising the role of state-led violence in the control of protesters. The decisive factor in Cairo was the refusal of the army to side with Hosni Mubarak against the people. But this restraint, however crucial, was perhaps motivated as much by cold calculation as by humanitarian concern; that in an age of greater openness and access to information, no regime can long survive if it massacres its own people to stay in power.

In 1989, China was still led by people who had fought in the bitter Sino–Japanese war of 1937–1945. They had real combat experience. Deng Xiaoping himself was known as a ruthless military commander who sacrificed huge numbers of lives to achieve battlefield victory. To him, the use of tanks against civilians in 1989 was not a problem.

More than two decades later, and even further from China's last experience of major conflict (the country's most recent significant military engagement was in February–March 1979, against Vietnam), it is critical to ask how much violence the current generation of leaders would be able to use in an emergency. Would the Chinese Communist Party's higher echelons really be able to deploy troops in the manner of 1989?

Egypt has shown China's political elite that even a well-funded, well-managed and well-connected army can disobey its political masters when it is ordered to turn fire on its own people. This is not a principle the Chinese Communist Party will want to test in practice. The likelihood must be that Beijing will continue the endless campaign of low-level repression and containment of social discontent — hoping in this way to avert the time when things get out of control.

China's Elite: A Language Deficit

8 February 2012

It was a bleak moment for the foreign-policy specialists in the central government in Beijing when US Secretary of State Hillary Clinton's plane touched down in Rangoon in early December 2011. For several years, China had been the one steadfast friend of Burma's ever-more isolated military regime. It was thus able to enjoy something approaching an economic monopoly there, even if India sought to press its interests in the resource-rich but isolated south Asian country.

Beijing had advance warning of an autumn chill when Barack Obama declared during his visit to Asia in late November that the US was, after its post-9/11 diversions in the Middle East and Afghanistan, now back and fully focused on its Pacific interests. For China, such sentiments evoke the fear that the US is becoming more involved than it would like in the affairs of its neighbours.

But the pattern is longer still. For in mid-2010, the US secretary of state said — in the context of flare-ups between Japan and China over disputed maritime borders — that both the South and East China Seas were legitimate areas of the US's strategic interest. Such consistency in the US's pronouncements and behaviour over the last 18 months suggests that it is indeed "back", strategically and psychologically, in east Asia. Many in Beijing see this refocus as an effort to thwart, frustrate and challenge a China that itself now has more ability to assert its key regional interests. The ingredients of China's calculations are familiar. They concern contests over borders and territory, access to economic and energy resources, and its capacity to influence the international system in ways the authorities in Beijing deem to its advantage.

Many high-level Chinese academics and officials regard the US's sheer ubiquity as almost a never-ending nightmare they hope one day to wake from. The US has a significant presence in South Korea, Japan and the Philippines. But more distressingly now, it is in places such as Vietnam (which could now obtain weapons from the US, something unthinkable even a few years ago), Pakistan and Mongolia. All around China's edges, it can seem from Beijing, the US seems to be cropping up — ever intent on a creeping mission of containment.

Only with regards to North Korea (the Democratic People's Republic of Korea; DPRK) can China feel any certainty that the US is absent — and even there, the leadership in Pyongyang harbours a deep-seated objective one day to negotiate directly with Washington. To put it another way, once the endless rhetoric of friendship fades, the shallowness of Chinese strategic alliances can appear both surprising and shocking.

This predicament is a clue to China's recent diplomatic behaviour, which has been a classic mixture of reassuring "peace-and-harmony speak" and permission to various agents of the central state to act with a sort of bolshie unilateralism. China's much-vaunted "peaceful rise" now includes sea-captains having brawls with South Korean, Japanese and Vietnamese vessels, and shrill denunciations of India for hosting the Dalai Lama (during the aborted first day of scheduled border talks, at the end of November 2011).

Such more combative behaviour in recent months can be seen as reflecting Beijing's frustration that its economic clout has outrun its political impact — and that its foreign-policy apparatus has simply been unprepared for the range and depth of questions that would confront it as it became an economic behemoth. In this perspective, China's fundamental policy stances — not seeking leadership, non-interference in the affairs of others — recall a time when it was an isolated and politically introspective country recovering from a devastating international and civil war, and obsessed with its endless domestic political campaigns. Today, in a world where China's footprint appears across the world, they are increasingly incongruous and ineffective. Yet no one in Beijing seems willing to challenge them, far less propose others adequate to the realities of 21st-century global politics.

The route to addressing the problem begins by acknowledging the obvious: that China — like every power — has legitimate international interests, but that it needs a far more convincing voice with which to express these. Its current leadership has been reluctant to, or simply incapable of, crafting a way of speaking to the world that ensures its words are believed and claims trusted. If China is worried about the prevalence of the US around its borders, then it needs to find a rhetoric — or perhaps better, a register — that enables it authentically to fight back. After all, as the Chinese themselves are fond of pointing out, Sun Zi stated over two millennium ago that the best victories are won before any physical conflict becomes necessary.

China's greatest disadvantage in this new war for international hearts and minds is its political model. Most of the rest of the world finds it outmoded and/or hard to understand, yet it is linked to a specific ideology and a language which governs the Chinese elite's modes of expression. China's politicians are thus saddled with a stiff and inexpressive vocabulary with which to talk to the outside world and their own people. If they were able to escape from it, many of China's demands as a country — its need for energy, concern over territory and fear of international containment — are easy enough to understand, even if disagreements over them continue (as is quite natural).

The new generation of Chinese leaders would do itself and the rest of the world a big favour if it revised and refreshed the stilted, highly unnatural way in which they talk about issues that matter to them. The world in 2012 awaits a Chinese leader with the ability to speak naturally and comfortably to the world. Perhaps only when he or she emerges will the US and others start both to take Beijing's legitimate fears more seriously and to engage in a proper discussion about what the balance of power and interest in Asia should be. Now that so much of the world's economic, political and military power is located there, that cannot happen soon enough.

China and Syria: A Question of Responsibility

With Cassidy Hazelbaker

2 April 2012

Over the last three decades, China has often been accused of amoral behaviour in its approach to international issues. Beijing, it is said, wants the trappings of a great power — ability to wield both soft and hard influence, while being respected and listened to — yet when difficult issues arise — both those that touch on its own interests and those that have no direct impact — it varies between indignantly proclaiming the importance of "non-interference in the affairs of others" and running as fast as it can from any responsibility.

Against this background, Syria represents the worst of all worlds for China. The state headed by Bashar al-Assad is not a key security ally of Beijing, a big supplier of energy, nor in any meaningful diplomatic or political sense a major partner. But it is an important country in a vital region, and China is fully aware that continued instability in Syria — of the kind that led to the toppling of regimes elsewhere in the Arab world — will greatly affect its interests. Moreover, China knows that the US, the European States and other powers are focusing attention on the crisis there (as in the conference in Istanbul on 1 April 2012), and posing questions to Beijing about its own stance.

The crisis in Syria erupted in February 2011 and quickly intensified as protests and repression spread across the country. The issue of humanitarian intervention soon came before the UN Security Council, only to be blocked by Russia's veto. China added its own veto to Moscow's, calculating that as the supportive player in a "group of two" on the council it would have at least some cover from criticism.

The furious response of the US secretary of state Hillary Clinton — who called China's stance "despicable" — made clear to China that its initial gambit of pairing off with Russia wasn't going to work. The vote on Syria was, after all, only the seventh time China has deployed its veto since it joined the UN system in 1971. By using it — rather than, as over Libya, simply abstaining — China was seen as sending a message. Russia's decision was expected since it has intimate diplomatic and security links with Syria, its one true ally in the Middle East. But China had other options. Why did it behave this way?

There are three probable reasons. The first is that China's authorities just don't buy the dominant Western-led discourse that regime change in Syria will improve the situation. They reject the depiction of the conflict in "good versus bad" terms and foresee a lengthy civil war in which the country will split and destabilise an already precarious region. The Syrian opposition is disorganised and disunited and even if the conference in Turkey results in greater coordination, the opposition is far from being able to lead the transition to a new government.

China also judges that Syria's sectarian politics still work overall in favour of the Assad regime, which retains much support from the Alawite community and from other minorities who fear the possible dynamics of a post-Assad order. These groups can justify their continuing support (or consent) by relying on the state-sponsored discourse that the violence in the country is being prompted by vicious rebel gangs as well as meddling foreigners.

The second reason for China's position is that it worries about the threat of "mission-creep" that follows intervention. Many Chinese officials argue that NATO's action in Libya in 2010–2011 went way beyond what had been originally foreseen. They now reflect that Beijing's abstention on the

UN Security Council vote on Libya opened the door to far wider US and European involvement than it had mandated or foreseen. The images of a bloodied Muammar Gaddafi being beaten and murdered after his capture in October 2011, which circulated widely in China, haven't helped. For the Chinese, this was not a just or dignified end to what had been labelled a necessary humanitarian intervention.

The third reason is even more potent: China's suspicion of the demand by Washington and its allies — voiced consistently over many years — that China should become a "stakeholder" in the international system. The Chinese elite increasingly suspects that this obscures a Western (and especially US) strategy to maintain dominance in the face of financial crisis and China's own rise, in which its strategic interests (in relation to maritime-border issues, for instance) are being constantly downgraded and sometimes thwarted. Why, Beijing wonders, should it become a "stakeholder" when every time it tries to promote its own case, much of the rest of the world starts shouting at it?

In this overall context, China's apparent passivity over Syria makes sense. So many questions surround the conflict there: over the outcome, whether what might follow Bashar al-Assad would be an improvement, the chances of a more extreme and disruptive regime coming to power, and the dangers of regional radicalisation. But the greatest problem in China's caution is that it has failed to propose a credible alternative plan to deal with this situation, beyond the idea of simply leaving people in Syria to sort out their own problems (and thus stand by as many are slaughtered).

Beijing knows what is happening in Syria is untenable and the comments of official spokespersons as former UN Secretary General and current peace envoy Kofi Annan arrived in China to garner support for his UN mission may indicate a slight adjustment of its view, if no guarantee of a change. But so far, it can't articulate an active but non-interventionist policy. At present, then, China's position — however it is explained and however logical it can look — lays it open to accusations of expediency and moral bankruptcy.

China rejects the role of stakeholder crafted for it from outside. But this still presents it with the challenge of finding the moral courage and strategic intelligence to develop a persuasive stance of its own when international crises arise. Syria remains an opportunity as well as a challenge for China. The world is waiting.

China and Japan: A Conflict of Logics

30 August 2012

The Chinese academic Zheng Wang has just published a book on historical memory and its role in China's politics and foreign affairs entitled *Never Forget National Humiliation*.[6] In it he writes that many outsiders have a "lack of understanding of the inner life of Chinese people". The government in Beijing may act as a mouthpiece for mainstream elite views, but what Chinese people themselves really think about current issues remains beyond the grasp of foreign observers even now, when social media has swamped both sides.

The spat that erupted in August 2012 between Japan and China over contested islets in the South China Seas (Senkaku/Diaoyu in the respective languages) might appear a perfect chance to remedy this situation — by seeing what blogs, internet postings and other new forums convey to non-Chinese about Chinese people's views on a sensitive national controversy. Even more so since, in relation to foreign affairs, Chinese people have some latitude to speak without agents of state "contaminating" their opinions with surveillance, official recriminations and censorship.

But here, too, it is advisable to bear Zheng Wang's caution in mind. The online sources contain a cacophony of opinion about Japan's "insults" (the vogue word) to China's territorial rights and national honour, and they are supplemented by equally angry demonstrations in Beijing and across the country against Japan (with targets from shops, businesses and cultural entities to Tokyo's diplomatic representatives). It is hard, though, to discern the "inner life of Chinese people" beneath the wealth of denunciation. In many ways, it can seem that Chinese public opinion in the social-media era has become more, not less, unknowable.

This matters because of the way that the Chinese government understands and seeks to support its national claims by reference to history and emotion. The contrast with the way Japan approaches the territorial dispute with China (one of several both countries are involved in with their

---

[6]Zheng Wang, *Never Forget National Humiliation*, Columbia University Press, New York, 2011.

neighbours) is clear. A senior official from Japan told me in July 2012 — before the latest escalation — that Japan understood well how it had to deal with China (which was shared by the rest of the world). In effect, you have a simple choice, the official said: either you give credence to China and its history-based claims — and thus have to deal with all the matters consequently arising (for example, what predecessor states existed before the current ones, how obligations and rights flow from one to the other, and where historic lines should be drawn) — or you conduct your diplomatic practice according to international law, basing everything on a recognition of the realities of current legal title and ownership.

The Japanese official implied that by China's logic, England's medieval ownership of lands in northern France could entitle the UK to make a valid territorial claim today, and that by any other logic, Japan was right in the dispute with China. The Japanese position, thus expressed, is at heart a straightforward play off between an emotional pre-modern territoriality (China) and rational modernity (Japan). As for the rest of the world, it should align its policy with its rhetoric, acknowledge that the Japanese stance was correct, then keep out.

China, for its part, could, with more dextrous diplomacy, advance its case over Diaoyu/Senkaku more persuasively to the outside world, while stirring a little less rancour (assuming these are among its wishes). A range of options are available under international law, which is after all an evolving body of work, including possible compromise short of a final settlement. In view of the latent resource conflicts in the disputed areas, most would want to see such an outcome in the short-to-medium term. Deng Xiaoping's advice over Taiwan in the 1980s remains apposite: the big issues about sovereignty can be kicked deep into the future, but the main thing now is to find a flexible way of working together which does not prejudge anything.

Today, China's leaders lack such pragmatism in comparable areas, and are prepared to allow hardline public expression to fuel their stance (though how far the elite knows what is in its citizens' minds is a question worth asking). This approach has its own costs. China's power is increasing, its voice in Europe and America is becoming more influential, its contribution to solving geopolitical problems is ever more needed. Amid such responsibilities, nasty rows with the neighbours strike a discordant note.

China could in principle choose to take a longer-term view, go for an interim solution to territorial spats, preserve good relations with its neighbours and continue the very successful economic path of recent decades. After all, it surely sees that the main beneficiaries of the current abrasive situation are the "China threat" peddlers, and that those who would depict its policy as driven by irrationality and emotion.

It is hard to see Japan backing down on the Diaoyu/Senkaku affair. Whether the nationalist Governor of Tokyo, Shintaro Ishihara, raises the money to buy them — his suggestion being the immediate cause of the latest row — or whether the Japanese government does so, Japanese ownership of them is not going to change. The policy of the Japanese authorities is to apprehend whoever comes towards the islands and send them home. So far, the country's Self Defence Forces have not been called on. But if they do get involved, then the most worrying of all outcomes begins to look possible — a military escalation between two countries with bitter and media-stoked memories of conflict.

The changes due within Japan and China in the next few months are the great variables here — China's leadership transition, which could either calm or amplify the voice of the nationalists and military, and the prospect of Japan's embattled Prime Minister Yoshihiko Noda (or his rivals) using a controversy like this for domestic purposes (possibly in an early election).

In this fluid period, it must be hoped that level heads and measured responses will prevail. But, where China is concerned, the country is no longer a struggling, impoverished local player but a powerful global actor. In matters of rocks as well as trade, currency and the environment, it needs to start acting like one, even when this requires leading rather than indulging "public opinion". When it really matters for the common good, after all, a government can change wars of public opinion. And on this matter, emotion or no emotion, the Chinese government really must.

Chapter Four

The Road to 2012: The Leadership Transition

Leadership transitions in China since 1949 have never been relaxing. As 2012 and an expected handover of Party and then government positions loomed, one of the common observations was that for Mao Zedong and Deng Xiaoping, they had been the ultimate headache. Mao's were the most unpleasant, with his first successor Liu Shaoqi felled in the Cultural Revolution of 1966 and dead within three years. The next, Lin Biao, was killed in a plane crash while fleeing the country in 1971. Others came and went, with the final choice, Hua Guofeng, referred to already, able to operate for only a few years before the resurgence of Deng Xiaoping. Deng's potential successors at least didn't lose their lives, though Hu Yaobang died of a heart attack in 1989, and Zhao Ziyang was placed under house arrest following his fall in May the same year.

Institutionalising leadership transitions was a big deal in China simply because of the need to avoid the appearance of an all-powerful political strong man like Mao Zedong. If there was one figure that captured the ambiguity of contemporary Chinese politics in the 21st century, the treatment of Mao was it. Lauded publicly, and loathed privately, smothered in the rhetoric used of a great man, but largely unheeded in terms of China's political and social development, Mao was no more than a symbolic figure and famously did not even feature in the 2008 Olympic opening ceremony. It was telling that in the second decade of the 21st century, the Chinese Communist Party still felt vulnerable to being taken over by an over-ambitious and power-focused individual. Hu acted at all times like the opposite of this — self-effacing, keeping a low profile, simply the CEO of a board united and acting as one.

Bo Xilai, who figures in several of the pieces in this chapter, aroused this deep antipathy to charismatic, driven political figures for the Chinese Communist Party, and his fall beginning at the start of 2012 became the biggest and most unexpected story of Chinese politics in a generation. Up to the end of 2011, he seemed to be cruising towards inevitable elevation from the full Politburo to the Standing Committee. An analyst airily told me in 2011 after meeting him that "he was too big to keep out, despite the fact that many like Wen Jiabao loathed him".

The analyst was right at least about the depth of loathing by Wen, for it was the usually avuncular Premier who delivered the coup de grace at the National People's Congress in 2012, signalling that Bo's time was up. He had no political future now that his chief security official Wang Lijun had disappeared to the US consulate in Chengdu for a day before being detained and hauled back to Beijing, and his wife had been formally indicted for the murder of a British businessman. Bo disappeared to be sentenced to life in prison in late 2013.

Bo's fall taught observers more about the workings of the elite of elites in the Chinese political system than any other event in the last few years. It was a rare opportunity to have a look in and see just how power was distributed, exercised and deployed in modern China. It showed that this was not a gentle or attractive system, and for all the mellifluous words used by figures like Hu and Wen about harmony and taking people as the key, when specific key interests were threatened, people could act with amazing brutality.

The great fear after Bo's fall was that the transition would end up being botched. Rumours abounded of Hu perhaps needing to stay on for several more years. There were claims that one of the members of the Standing Committee under Hu, Zhou Yongkang, was in deep trouble because of his anger at the way Bo had been treated. The disappearance for a fortnight of Xi Jinping in September 2012 ratcheted anxiety up even further, with a plethora of claims that he was either suffering from a swimming accident, injuries from an assassination attempt or from a car crash.

The transition, in the end, did happen, and with a whimper rather than a bang. On 15 November 2012, seven men strolled out in the Great Hall of the People, and the end of Hu's period as Party Secretary had finally arrived. Ironically, the fact that the transition had been achieved despite a number of uneasy moments and threats may well go down as one of Hu's most significant achievements. In a system where precedent is crucial, this changeover of leaders without the looming ghost of a political godfather like Deng Xiaoping is hugely useful. What is less clear is how, in the coming decade, a whole new generation of leaders will step in when Xi Jinping and Li Keqiang come to the end of their terms. But that is, happily, the subject of other books by other people in another time.

China's Next Elite: 2012 and Beyond

With Loh Su-Hsing

16 August 2010

It is a commonplace to state that the relationship between the US and the People's Republic of China is the most important single bilateral relationship in the world in the early 21st century. It is less observed that in autumn 2012, both countries — and not just the former — will be undergoing the vital process of choosing the political leadership to guide them through the next years. It is another commonplace that the outcome in the US matters hugely to the world as well to America itself. China's global rise means that in 2012, more than ever before, the same is true of the contest in Beijing.

The way the leadership is selected in the two states is a lesson in political difference. The contrasts of process are highlighted in the very public positioning in which candidates for the US presidency must indulge, and in the incumbent's attempts to create the most favourable climate for his re-election. The contest between Barack Obama and his Republican opponent will be a popular election full of high drama (with elements of a soap opera too), funded by vast donations, waged on the 24/7 media and tracked by constant polling.

In China, the method of selection resembles more a lengthy game of chess, full of a million understated and opaque tactical decisions, and is everything but public. When the members of the new Chinese Communist Party leadership walk out from behind the curtain of the Great Hall of the People in late 2012 — including the successors of Hu Jintao and Wen Jiabao — the result of that epic, intricate chess game will finally be known.

There are a vast number of studies of political leadership in America. But how do you become a leader in China today? What do you have to do?

Who has to like you and support you, and who do you have to defeat? What are the rules within which you live your life?

The initial thing to note is that Chinese politicians come from a singularly narrow background. They share much of the same experience, inhabit the same ideological universe and tend to live and work in close proximity to each other. Where Western politicians are desperate most of the time to show that they are "one of us", leaders in China are always and forever "one of them" — members of a tightly defined group, where the golden rule seems to be not to stand out too much.

The 18th National Congress of the Chinese Communist Party — the 17th was held in October 2007 — will be a hugely significant moment for China. The country's most powerful figures will (according to rules the current leadership itself devised) retire. As many as seven of the Politburo's nine-member Standing Committee will leave the stage, including Hu Jintao, Wen Jiabao and Wu Bangguo. It is almost certain that Xi Jinping will succeed Hu as President and Party Secretary, and that Li Keqiang will succeed Wen as Premier; but some key positions in the Standing Committee are the subject of intense speculation, and the full Politburo will be full of new faces.

In seeking to understand this process, the greatest problem is that there are no clear frameworks. In democratic states there are political parties; government and opposition; left and right currents; and open media. In the world's last major one-party state none of this applies. In recent years, analysts of China have come to employ notions of "populists" and "elitists", and to talk of affiliation to particular factions (such as the "Shanghai group"). But these markers seem less reliable today.

In part this is because China's current generation of leaders seem more homogenous than any previous one. These leaders have no experience of pre-1949 China, are products of the Cultural Revolution era of 1966–1976 and are wholly formed by the culture of the Chinese Communist Party. The overall result is an appearance of facelessness and uniformity. The most distinctive feature in its way is one that actually links China to the West: the rule of technocrats is ending, and that of lawyers and political scientists coming to ascendancy.

China's present crop of leaders differs from its predecessors too in its lack of international experience. This could represent a real problem, for the rising importance and strength of China in all domains mean that the country's national leadership now also has global significance. The person who leads China from 2012 will be a major international political player, more than Hu Jintao has been. In this respect, the successor generation looks deficient.

Chinese communist leaders, reflecting what their political system has required of them, tend to lack charisma, communication skills and an aptitude for public engagement. They follow the Party line in all public appearances, deliver speeches that are rehearsed and formulaic, and remain formal and distant in personal interactions. All this reinforces an impression of an indistinguishable elite lacking individual personality — faceless even to the domestic populace and distantly homogeneous to the rest of the world. It is worth noting that only Li Yuanchao, Li Keqiang and Bo Xilai of the full Politburo are fluent in English, all but one (Zhang Dejiang) of the current Politburo were solely educated in China with no period of studying abroad, and that none of the 62 provincial chiefs (the party secretaries and governors, from which the majority of future national leaders usually come) have received an academic degree outside of China.

The leadership that will assume central power in autumn 2012 — part of the generation whose education was disrupted by the chaotic years of the Cultural Revolution — will therefore face intense critical questioning about its capacity to manage the immense problems that will confront the country they will be taking charge of. China's next decade is going to be very difficult; the huge challenges will include securing legitimacy among an increasingly restless Chinese public, and outlining a vision for China that can have appeal both domestically and throughout the rest of the world. The nature of the leadership-transition process means that China's prospective rulers, who are already in the midst of a battle for preferment, need publicly give no indication of their preferred plans for the country before being elevated to the summit of power. That all happens afterwards.

What makes it harder for the next Beijing elite is that standing still is not an option. The international demands placed upon China are becoming more pressing and multifaceted, the aspirations of the population higher and (in line with its changing profile) diverse. The Communist Party too, whose survival over the two post-cold-war decades reflects its adaptability as well as tenacity, must evolve correspondingly. The overriding need over the next decade is for a reinvigorated leadership that understands its own changing society and is at home in the world. To meet it, the Party faces an imminent challenge now: to cast aside its inherent conservatism and start promoting cadres in their 30s and 40s to more senior positions. This unavoidable test raises a prospect that shadows the great chess game of 2012. In 2017 or 2022 a raft of new, younger, more internationally minded figures from within China need to be found to become the country's leaders. The whole notion of leadership within the country needs to be radically reformulated and altered. The world faces the real prospect of then dealing not with a contemporary Mao Zedong — but with China's indigenous version of a Bill Clinton or Tony Blair. The question will then be not only whether the Chinese people are ready for this, but also whether we outsiders are up to it too.

China's Great Transition: The Next Party Congress

29 July 2011

A public furore is continuing in China over the accident on 23 July 2011 involving a collision between two of the country's new high-speed trains near the eastern city of Wenzhou, Zhejiang province, which killed 40 people. The early response of the authorities to the disaster, combining scant information and a perfunctory investigation, has provoked intense criticism. The Premier, Wen Jiabao, was obliged to make a belated visit to the scene and expressed the government's intention to undertake a thorough inquiry.

The episode is all the more telling as it comes at the end of a month when the ruling Chinese Communist Party has been celebrating the 90th anniversary of its foundation in 1921. A range of official events and ceremonies, films and exhibitions, programmes and publications have marked the moment, and the Party's economic and social achievements — including the rapid construction of fast new railway lines across the country — feature prominently.

Even as its ripples still reverberate, the affair tells much about the nature of power in China and — a recurrent theme throughout this book — the problems the Chinese Communist Party has in governing a society in ferment. In the context of the rail accident, the way the Party has represented its history in July 2011 reveals anew the scale of the task it faces.

The Chinese Communist Party's official version of its own history — finally published after almost a decade of writing, rewriting, revising and perfecting — is monumental: almost 1,000 pages across two volumes. And this, it has to be remembered, only covers three of the Party's nine decades: from 1949, when the Chinese Communist Party won the Civil War and came to power, to 1978, the dawn of the reform and opening-up era which continues to this day. This, then, is the history of the Chinese Communist Party under Mao Zedong (who died in September 1976). The continuing controversy over the true role of Mao and a proper assessment of him in China is the reason even writing such a work posed a huge challenge, and why its appearance is meaningful.

The Chinese Communist Party's own celebration of its 90th birthday took place on 1 July 2011. The Party Secretary Hu Jintao — who, like Wen Jiabao, will pass the baton to his successor in 2012 — spoke to the Party's 80 million current members. He reflected on the transformation of a political force that had started with a clandestine meeting of just 11 people in 1921 in Shanghai, and that now enjoys command of the world's second-largest economy. Hu talked proudly of the Chinese Communist Party's long record of success — including victory in the 1937–1945 war against the Japanese (which was shared with the nationalist Kuomintang, though the key role of the Kuomintang in victory during this is only recently being properly acknowledged in the People's Republic), unification of the country and the inauguration of economic reform in the late 1970s.

The very fact that this official history of the Chinese Communist Party is so limited in scope serves to highlight how contentious the earlier era was and remains. Only two of those 11 attendees in Shanghai (Mao Zedong himself and Dong Biwu) ended their natural lives in the Chinese Communist Party fold; the other nine were murdered, exiled or expelled. Whatever else its rewards, founding a Marxist party in China was not for those in search of a safe or quiet life.

The rise of Mao to power is an especially sensitive issue of the post-1921 period. The Chinese Communist Party's use of violence and coercion under his leadership is one of the great untold stories of the People's Republic of China and at the moment, remains largely unwritable through lack of proper archival access. One day, the central archives in Beijing may share their secrets (like other authoritarian systems, the Chinese Communist Party has been a scrupulous record keeper), but that is unlikely to happen any time soon.

But the Party has had many difficulties too in dealing with the 1949–1978 era. Since 1980, there has been political sanction to criticise the Cultural Revolution (1966–1976) as a disaster for the Chinese Communist Party and the country that was brought about by Mao's mistakes, though Mao's overall contribution is still venerated. The residual respect for Mao was recently on show at the "red song" campaigns championed by Bo Xilai, Party Secretary of the vast city-province of Chongqing; and reflected in a book about the Chinese Communist Party for foreign readers by Li Junru, former Deputy Head of the Central Party School (the Chinese Communist Party's main think tank), which describes Mao as a "genius and a great man who will never be forgotten by the Chinese". Those who attack Mao's legacy do so at their own peril; the writer Mao Yushi, for example, received death threats after publishing an article critical of the "great helmsman".

More broadly, the Chinese Communist Party seems to be going through a third moment — after 1942 and 1980 — of reflection and stocktaking. These earlier occasions came at the point of a historic shift, when (in 1942), the Party needed to re-evaluate its anti-Japanese military strategy and (in 1980) had to shape the reform process. The equivalent change this time is twofold. First, the Chinese Communist Party is undergoing a major leadership transition in which as much as two-thirds of its elite leaders (those at director-general level and above) are about to retire. A new generation will take over following the Party Congress in 2012 (see "China's Next Elite: 2012 and Beyond", 16 August 2010; in this volume, pp. 79–82).

Second, China is entering a phase of huge transformation, with a booming economy and dynamic society bringing new forces and challenges into play. Again, the government's panicky reaction to the rail accident in Zhejiang is revealing. In the age of the internet and 24/7 media, and of an increasingly educated and aware population, the old Maoist-era "supervision of mass opinion" approach doesn't stand a chance.

Most observers of the "red song" campaigns realise that they were merely nostalgic exercises with zero political meaning. Chinese citizens are becoming as demanding, fussy, complaining and irritable as people anywhere else on the planet. Beyond anniversaries and other staged events, the Chinese Communist Party is embarked on a vast exercise to keep them content, to administer them efficiently, and to prove it is their best guarantor of a stable, prosperous and stronger China in the years ahead.

The Chinese Communist Party must change — and to their credit, its leading officials and most of its members know that. By the time it marks its centenary in 2021, it will face some tough decision-points when major issues need to be clarified — about the speed of political reform, the role of the rule of law and of civil society and the contract between the state and citizens. To meet them, the Party has to modernise by becoming more transparent, accountable, and better able to discipline and manage its own members.

The Three Rules of Chinese Politics

4 October 2011

A major leadership transition in China is expected a year from now. As I write, things are happening in Beijing — deals being started, in progress, going wrong — which we are likely to learn of only a long time into the future (and perhaps not even then). The current power-play will help decide the identity of the 11 or so real contenders for the (probable) seven available positions on the all-important Standing Committee of the Politburo, the summit of power in the contemporary People's Republic of China. Chinese politics often seem opaque and mysterious; "byzantine" in the all-purpose formula. It is helpful then to recall that there are several ground rules. Here are three that might shed light on the leadership process.

The first rule of contemporary Chinese politics relates to the nature of the Chinese system, which is true to its Soviet roots in the sense of being rationalist. It follows procedures based on the notion of human perfectibility and logicalness. This is both its greatest strength — because it gives everything the veneer of planning and control — and its greatest weakness — because humans can hardly ever live up to what the system expects of them.

In practice this means that there will be a reason behind each person's final arrival on the Standing Committee. In Chinese politics there is always a cause-and-effect explanation, connected usually to the dense networks and links between people, factions, groups and social worlds. True, even the keenest observer of Chinese politics can only imperfectly understand the ups and the downs. But the first rule is that if things look odd, we just haven't been able to look far enough under the table to work them out; if we could, everything would make perfect sense.

The second rule follows on from these networks and links, and from how complicated the calculations are over who gets lifted up and who loses out. This system is less about individuals than about the extended circles of patronage, vested interest and family around them. This makes preferment also a matter of appealing to the interests of as wide a constituency as possible; and that involves material, and sometimes financial, inducements. It's not that getting onto the Standing Committee is a function of being able to spend or promise as many billions of *yuan* as candidates in the US can pledge dollars. But it is about whose ascent will bring gain to many others, and what sort of worlds — state-owned businesses, military top brass, political elites, even academic and cultural centres — these might be from.

In a system in which the highest official in the Chinese Communist Party gets — on paper at least — only a few hundred dollars a month, real transparency is a daydream. In crude terms, elevation to the Politburo Standing Committee might not gain the winning candidate immediate riches, but it will bring their wide networks into a hitherto almost unimaginable world of wealth. For these, a link with the winners of the leadership transition is akin to a connection within a multi-trillion-dollar business. The second rule of contemporary Chinese politics, therefore, is to follow the money.

The third rule is about the political hierarchy at the very top level. Most of the excited speculation concerns who will succeed Hu Jintao as Party Secretary or Wen Jiabao as Premier; very little focuses on the second position in the Standing Committee order. Yet the occupant of this slot — currently the largely unknown Wu Bangguo — has the critical role of responsibility for China's nominal parliament, the National People's Congress. If a reformist lands this position in late 2012, then the moment he walks out from behind the curtain we will know whether this is a leadership prepared, at some point, to make the congress genuinely more representative; and if the answer is yes, we will know that the era of socio-political change has at last arrived. The third rule of modern Chinese politics, therefore, is never forget number two![1]

---

[1] In fact, this rule was promptly subverted when Li Keqiang as Premier was made number two in the Politburo hierarchy. Even so, this raised interesting questions about what sort of different powers and influences he would have in this position compared to his predecessor Wen, who only ranked third.

It is unusual to reduce Chinese politics to these basic precepts. But the approach is also one way to access the reality of an unusual system; one that seems to have little to do with the individual personalities or qualities of those involved. The upper echelons of the People's Republic of China are now full of competent administrators with a wide range of skills that, however, they hardly ever need to demonstrate in public. The system's key requirement is elsewhere: to align the immense configuration of economic, political and power interests that it embodies to ensure its stability for (at least) the next five years.

The stakes are high. The rewards of power in modern China are huge, almost beyond imagining, but the costs of failure are cataclysmic. This is where the weight really does fall on individuals, for if you mess up, your career — and its benefit for those in your universe — comes to a shuddering halt. The great exception here was Deng Xiaoping, who returned from political oblivion to become architect of the reform process that shaped the country's three decades of transformation. It will not happen again, and all involved in the leadership transition know it. Here is the fourth unwritten rule of modern Chinese politics: there are no second acts.

China's Party, Bo Xilai's Legacy

With David Goodman

5 May 2012

Every society has its defining moments, and China is no exception to the rule. In recent decades alone there has been the death of Mao Zedong in 1976, the start of reform under Deng Xiaoping in 1978, the Tiananmen incident of 1989 and the Olympic Games of 2008. Now, the dismissal of the high-profile politician Bo Xilai in 2012 is and will be remembered as an event of equivalent significance.

The fall of Bo Xilai marks a new phase of how the Chinese Communist Party does politics and communicates with the Chinese public. Bo's biggest legacy to the Party will relate less to the corruption and over-ambition that caused his exit, for these already have precedents in its upper reaches. His real gift will turn out to be to force the leadership to speak in a new way and relate differently to Chinese people. In itself this will be transformational.

This might seem an exaggerated claim, especially based on what little is known so far: that Bo Xilai has been suspended from membership of the Party and the Politburo, and thus his once glittering career is shattered. It is also true that the Chinese Communist Party's disciplinary procedures have permitted reversal of such verdicts in the past. But that was a long time ago; in Chinese politics after Deng Xiaoping, there are no second acts.

The scale of the change underway can be measured by two aspects of the story. The first is the way the Bo Xilai affair touches on China's power-elite. Bo was himself a rising star within this elite: a charismatic, handsome and able son of a leader of the 1949 revolution who had moved up the political hierarchy to lead Chongqing, a massive provincial-level city in south-west China. There he implemented an approach to social and economic development that was at odds with China's orthodoxy since 1989, emphasising the state and social development more than the market and economic goals *per se.*

A key part of this policy orientation was a political-communication strategy that enlisted the emotional pull of "red songs" unheard since their heyday in the late Maoist period. The public seemed enthusiastic both about the improvements to their lives and the choral accompaniment. By the end of 2011, it seemed certain that Bo Xilai had the momentum to secure a place on the Standing Committee of the Politburo — the summit of China's new leadership — which was to be chosen in late 2012.

But in early February 2012, the sudden flight of Chongqing's Police Chief, Wang Lijun — once Bo's most trusted lieutenant — to the US consulate in neighbouring Chengdu punctured his progress. Wang took with him documents which (he claimed) contained evidence to disgrace Bo Xilai and his family. The defection, albeit short-lived, was the prelude to a cascade of charges of corruption, torture and violence under Bo's administration of Chongqing. The revelations inevitably tarnished the image of a national leadership that, since the elevation of Hu Jintao and Wen Jiabao in 2002, has managed to preserve itself from scandalous exposure of this kind.

The second aspect of the Bo Xilai story is its implications for the conduct of political communications within the People's Republic of China. The leadership of the Party has tried to handle the drama through the usual mechanisms of management and control. It formally announced that Bo Xilai, pending investigation in late March, was to be suspended as a Party member. Then, through inner-party briefings, it made clear that he would be disciplined. This was reinforced by the state media in the familiar, regimented way.

This time, however, there has been strong resistance both to the message and the process, and not just from those who supported what Bo Xilai stood for in Chongqing but more widely across the internet, social media and even in the less-official print media. The proponents of accountable politics contend that this is a revengeful power struggle rather than a contest about justice. This counter current is so fierce that, in a remarkable development, the Party was forced on 19 April to respond. The official state news agency published a commentary proclaiming that "criminal cases should not be interpreted as political struggle" and that Bo Xilai is being investigated for "disciplinary violations".

This degree of additional elaboration is unprecedented; the signal of a desire for greater legitimacy. In the old days, the Party said things once and that was it. Now it has to argue its case.

Just as striking, however, is that it may well not be enough. The Party's handling of Bo's dismissal has increased both awareness of and cynicism about the conduct of politics in China. Bo Xilai and the politics of his downfall are being discussed everywhere — and many, far more numerous than his sympathisers, believe that he has been "framed". They hold that the way his dismissal has been handled indicates that the Party remains addicted to old-fashioned power politics, and is visibly unable to adapt to manage (let alone to lead) the new era of political communications.

The leadership around Hu Jintao has until now performed in a disciplined, regulated and unified way. This has led some to see the Bo Xilai drama as a clever plan hatched by the President and his supporters to take out a rival. But it is far more likely that they were as surprised as anyone, and as little in charge. For today, Hu and his colleagues face similar problems to those of Barack Obama and other Western leaders — governing without being able to control either the message or the messenger, and being obliged increasingly to negotiate with a complex and greatly diversified public and media world.

Bo Xilai was the first of the new generation to experiment with a more personal, emotional way of speaking to China's people. If the leaders that remain want to secure their legitimacy for very much longer, they will need to learn some of his skills.

Chongqing and Bo Xilai: How China Works

16 August 2012

At night, approached from a certain direction, the city of Chongqing in China's south-west looks a little like Hong Kong. Its city centre lies on a promontory, with its skyscrapers, blazing with light, rising impressively over the surrounding water. By day, any such illusions tend to be shattered. In the early 2000s, soon after Chongqing was granted special status as a municipality directly under the central government — and thus separated from the vast Sichuan province — the city became known as one of China's most polluted places. One informal estimate said it enjoyed only 17 days of sunlight a year. The rest of the time it was under an enveloping man-made toxic fog.

Around the same time, in 2004, the city acquired the title of the world's largest conurbation, with a population in excess of 30 million. The more sceptical observers worked out that this had to be spurious. Chongqing covered an area the size of most British counties, or the smaller of American states. Even to describe it as a city would be a stretch. The urban area of Chongqing that most outsiders encountered gave a misleading impression: most of the rest of the "city" looked like contemporary rural areas elsewhere in the People's Republic of China.

I visited Chongqing in 2007, a few months before Bo Xilai was sent there as Party Secretary following a surprise decision at the 17th Party Congress of the Chinese Communist Party in Beijing. Like many others, I was enthused and intrigued by reports that the city — renowned throughout the world as "Chunking" — was making efforts to rebrand itself and attract international visitors. I met with members of the local government's information office, who showed me flashy presentations about how Chongqing would project itself as "a place where everyone can come" (in Chinese, the strapline was *ren ren lai Chongqing*).

The equivalent of the city's tourist bureau had created pleasant little lapel badges showing two figures walking, a symbol of how the world was about to beat a track to Chongqing's door. Direct flights from Europe and elsewhere in Asia to the newly built airport at the suburb of Jiangbei offered a fresh target market and entry point. Chongqing was about to have a second lease of life. It would, one of the officials declared to me, become "the Hong

Kong of the mainland"; indeed, one of the slick, professional adverts showed a visitor flying in for a weekend and experiencing a moment of revelation: this city was everything Hong Kong had wanted, and failed, to be!

Chongqing now, in 2012, presents a more complicated face to the world. The high-profile Bo Xilai did indeed make waves, following the pattern of his term of office in Dalian in China's north-east by waging noisy campaigns, attracting attention and telling the world this was the place to come — if only for an audience with the great rising star. But Chongqing's underside was never far away and could not easily be hidden. It was a city riddled with illegal activity, where mafia traded in contraband goods and ran large swathes of the local economy, almost heedless of the writ of the Party.

Bo had the political guts to deal with this, but the outcomes weren't pretty. He fought the mafia by subverting due process. A lawyer, for example, was badly beaten up and then detained without explanation when trying to represent some of those accused of mafia activity; a large number of business people was rounded up and given a form of summary justice without a clear sense of what they were being accused of. A climate of fear grew, and was strong enough to reach the foreign press. Bo countered the whiff of violence that attached to him with can-do showmanship. Here, was the message, is a man at last trying to clean up the city, deal with illegal bandits and, in the process, address social problems of inequality and sustainable housing. Even if it was all a bit rough and ready, Bo — went the narrative — wasn't just drifting with the wind but trying to *achieve* something.

Perhaps he was. But when in February 2012 his security chief, a man reportedly at the heart of the brutal treatment of some of the local mafia, made a spectacular attempt to claim asylum in the US consulate in nearby Chengdu, things began to unravel. Chongqing, the aspirant to becoming a second Hong Kong — a centre of trade, tourism, international travel and investment — was reverting to a furnace of overheated conspiracy, deadly conflict and bitter court intrigues. Bo's wife Gu Kailai was directly implicated in the death in November 2011 of a British businessman, Neil Heywood, and the great man himself was summarily suspended first from his Chongqing post, then from his position on the Politburo, his prospects of advancement to the very top leadership in China's forthcoming transition (or any subsequent one) almost certainly terminated.

For many, the grim theatre around Bo and his wife's fall only underlines that the more things change in China, the more they stay the same. In the end, this is a system predicated on unaccountable power, where at the heart of governance a few all-important individuals engage in coalition building and mutual support to advance each other's interests without input from public opinion. A crucial factor in this respect was that Bo lacked anyone in the Standing Committee of the Politburo who was willing to take a risk and support him. That, more even perhaps than the misdemeanours of his wife and family, sealed his fate.

Chongqing today seems a more uneasy, even sinister, place than before the waves of scandal broke. Those who suffered during the anti-mafia crackdown are recounting their stories of abuse during that period. It is a time of recrimination. Suddenly it is acceptable to say the previously unsayable — that Bo Xilai, the Party secretary, was out of control and practising his own form of illegality. It's probably more accurate to say that one form of confusion has been replaced by another. For Bo's treatment is about as political as it can get in the contemporary People's Republic of China. Anything touched by him has implications for the current leaders and their self-interest, in conditions where truth is but a variable. The inner circle's key concern is to prevent any contagion from Bo's case affecting them.

What really happened in the room of the bitterly misnamed Lucky Holiday Inn where Neil Heywood died in November, who did what, and what the link with Bo Xilai was — all this might never be known. Beyond the private tragedy, however, the saddest thing about this case is that even if the full truth were told, it is very unlikely it would be believed. In that sense, China's communist leadership have created for themselves and for the Chinese people a prison far harder to escape from than the one in which Chongqing's mafia were held.

Bo Xilai's Fall: Echo and Portent

12 October 2012

Who could have expected any other outcome to the Bo Xilai affair? After all, the path of the well-connected former boss of Chongqing, from contender for the Standing Committee of the Politburo of the Chinese Communist

Party to political oblivion, took the same course as every other elite career in China in the last two decades that was interrupted by scandal or disgrace.

The choreography was striking. When, on 28 September 2012, the official Xinhua news agency formally announced the date of the long-awaited 18th Party Congress where China's top leadership for the next five years (and possibly decade) would be chosen, the news was accompanied by a statement confirming Bo's expulsion from the Chinese Communist Party. The wording was unambiguous, and alongside references to corruption and larceny were accusations of illicit relations with women. For those following the arcane language of high-level Chinese politics, this could mean only one thing: that the final vestiges of protection were gone, and Bo was now going to be exposed to attack over every aspect of his personal and public life. Politically, he is dead, and the time for rumours about some kind of a comeback are over.

What does the treatment of Bo Xilai reveal about the particular configurations of power and its dynamics in modern China? The most powerful message may be that "the more things change, the more they stay the same". For, in the year since the scandal exploded with the dramatic flight of Bo's Police Chief and ally Wang Lijun to the US consulate in Chengdu (supposedly armed with a damning dossier), the ghosts of earlier power struggles have hovered eerily around this story.

Some are more recent than others: the serpentine movements against disgraced figures such as Chen Liangyu in Shanghai in 2006–2007, or even Chen Xitong in Beijing a decade before. But it is a far older parallel that keeps coming into view: the case of Lin Biao, deputy and chosen successor of Mao Zedong when the Cultural Revolution was in full swing in the late 1960s.

The similarities shouldn't be overstated. Lin Biao was no Bo Xilai, and the context of their respective falls from grace is very different. But in the firmament of allegations against Bo there are echoes of those attached to Lin after he fled China in 1971 on a jet-plane — reputedly *en route* to the Soviet Union — which crashed across the border in the Mongolian People's Republic. There followed suggestions that Lin had been agitating for an internal uprising (earlier troop and aircraft movements in Beijing and Shanghai were used as further confirmation).

The arguments against the discredited Bo also resemble those directed at Lin. Just as Lin was said to have been willing to challenge the mighty Mao, the narrative was that Bo's hubris had grown so great as to embolden him to strike at the most powerful figures in the land. Even the portrayal of Bo's wife Gu Kailai — now convicted of the murder of the businessman Neil Heywood — has close similarities to that of Lin Biao's partner Ye Qun, also reputed to be consumed by an epic ambition that made her the real driver of the drama.

The greatest parallel, however, is in the aftermath. By 1972, a few months after Lin's fall, his once ubiquitous name had simply and without explanation disappeared. It was only in the final weeks of 1972 that a dossier of material was produced (initially for Party workers, then for the wider public) and consumed with a mix of incredulity and bewilderment.

The documents were blood curdling. A man who had been regarded as Chairman Mao's true heir and successor, spoken of in the most flowery language of which Chinese communist hagiography was capable, was now portrayed as a traitor, a renegade and a hoodlum, guilty of the worst misdemeanours, such as linking with treacherous foreign forces, watching corrupt foreign films and harbouring mistresses. Yet in the context of this late period of Maoist excess, the Chinese public's reception of these charges was far from straightforward, and it was probably the treatment of Lin that led eventually to the demonstrations in Beijing in 1976, months before Mao's death in September of that year, and the swift repudiation of his mode of rule that ensued.

In the case of Bo too, his suspension from Party positions in April 2012 and removal as Party boss of Chongqing was followed by a period of official silence. The main mode of attack has been by proxy, via the murder trial of his wife Gu Kailai and his Security Chief Wang Lijun (who was sentenced in September 2012 to 15 years in jail for treachery). These indirect assaults created the mood music for the final exclusion of Bo from public life. Now, as with Lin Biao, it will be open season, and the very different Chinese public of 2012 will be exposed to a sordid portrait of the venality, corruption and immorality of Bo's life as a would-be leader of contemporary China.

Here, the current leadership has a twofold problem. The first is that, compared to Mao's time, the Chinese people's receptiveness to absolutist morality tales of once good and proper leaders turned unspeakably bad is now almost non-existent. Most citizens might be prepared to tolerate for a while the official version of the amazing Chonqqing drama, though more because its events and characters seem so far from the daily economic concerns that dominate their lives; but the notion that they will internalise the fairytale of a wicked Bo who had concealed his real nature for so long — and of a good Party that exposed him — is stretching things too far.

The second problem, however, is exactly the same as it was in Mao's time. It can be expressed as a question: if Lin Biao or Bo Xilai was so terrible, so wicked, so bad, then why is it that you — the Chinese Communist Party leadership — were happy to have him amongst you for so long, and speak of him so well? It is not so far from this to the conclusion that the real issue is not about Lin or Bo, but about *you*; your failure to acknowledge reality, your willingness to tolerate someone so dangerous, your lack of concern for and even complicity in the crimes you now denounce. On this question and the dangerous trail of thought it opens, the Party is so far silent.

Chapter Five

The Enemies Within: Separatists, Dissidents, and the Protestors

Harmonious China puzzled those that visited it with its raw anarchic energy. That politicians needed to stress the importance of harmony alerted the more observant to the fact that there were deep anxieties running through the very fabric of Chinese society that were becoming more unmanageable by the day. This has been alluded to already in the steep increases in internal security spending outlined in Chapter One. It had also loomed over the Olympics, with the Tibet uprising of early 2008 which had overshadowed some of the preparations for this event.

2009 was to be no easier. While China fought off the impact of the deteriorating international economic situation, it also had to face down a second bout of severe unrest in Xinjiang, an autonomous region taking up 18% of China's landmass but with a highly contested relationship to the central government. Xinjiang and Tibet were joined by unrest in the less-high-profile Inner Mongolian region in 2011. These three great regions covering the west, north-west and north-eastern borders of the People's Republic of China, were politically, economically and historically important, because sovereignty over them and stable governance of them in an integrated country were critical pillars for the Communist Party's claims to legitimate rule.

Those, internally or externally, who used these regions to question this issue of legitimacy for the Chinese Communist Party were straying into one of the most treacherous and dangerous areas. Figures like Hada, referred to in this chapter, or Gao Zhisheng were the martyrs in this territory; people who unleashed through their actions and questions the full force of the party-state, which either imprisoned, silenced or otherwise dealt with them. This dark side of modern Chinese state behaviour was uncomfortable to talk about, but often unavoidable. The brute fact was that a Party which had risen to power on the back of violent revolution and struggle was still, in the era of late modernity, willing to use distressing levels of coercion and violence — even if largely out of sight — against those who opposed it and caused it trouble.

None of the rights cases discussed here are straightforward. It is deeply puzzling why Gao Zhisheng was considered such a threat that he was detained and victimised in the ways described below. Someone who had met him in the late 2000s before he was "disappeared" said he seemed to have a martyr complex. Even so, his case raises some of the most difficult questions for the treatment of dissidents and the delivery of justice in modern China. Whatever his psychological state, the ways in which he was treated cannot be considered dignified and just in any system, let alone one in which its main political leaders preach harmony. The simple conclusion from all of this was that China's leaders might deploy the vocabularies of balance, justice and progress, but high-profile cases of punishment and torture of figures like Gao fundamentally undermined what they said. Were they powerless to restrain their own agents or did they, in fact, feel this was the right course of action to take? Elite politicians in the People's Republic of China never made themselves available to be asked this sort of detailed question, taking refuge in generalities and platitudes. But it was questions like this that refused to disappear.

Liu Xiaobo, the Nobel Prize laureate who was in prison from late 2009, figures greatly in the pieces that follow simply because his writings offered the most forensic moral critique of the contemporary Chinese Communist Party power system. For this reason, they had very particular use and force. There were many questions too about precisely why Liu was treated in the way he was, despite the reputational harm this did to China, and the fact that there was little in his political proposals that, at least on the surface, the Party opposed. Was he being held up as an example to scare others off, or was his treatment in some ways a sign of profound weakness in the leadership?

Debates about values and rights in Chinese society over the period 2007–2013 grew almost impossibly complex. No one could deny that Chinese citizens were more rights conscious and that when they expressed anger over food safety or mainstream issues like this, the government had to have a response. Social media was developing in ways that were simply

unforeseen before 2000, with a wholly new dynamic operating, showing
the complexity and diversity of Chinese public opinion. Those that airily
referred to what Chinese believed or thought as though there was some
elemental unity were confronted with a complete cacophony of different
opinions and ideas in cyberspace. This, more than anything else, became
an extraordinary map of contention in Chinese society, a space where some
of the issues of conflict, dissonance and disharmony referred to here and in
previous chapters could almost be physically seen.

Xinjiang: China's Security High Alert

14 July 2009

In summer 1995, I spent six weeks wandering around Xinjiang. It wasn't an
easy place to get through at that time. A three-day train ride from Beijing to
Urumqi was followed by another three days on the "luxury bus" that set off
from Urumqi centre and ended up, a thousand bumps later, in the market
place at Kashgar. This was several years before a new railway line linked
the most western city in China, almost on the Pakistan border, to the rest of
the People's Republic of China.

Kashgar was like nowhere else in China. Only a fraction of the local
inhabitants were Han Chinese. The city was dominated by a mosque and the
food, language and feel of the place were wholly different to other Chinese
cities (apart, rather tellingly, from Lhasa in Tibet, whose exotic atmosphere
and local colour, albeit very different in content, it shared).

My abiding memory of that long trip was the intractable complexity
of Xinjiang. A fifth of China's landmass, with endless kilometres of high-
altitude grassland, and over 20 different ethnic groups, there was already —
even in 1995 — a sense of edginess and unresolved, perhaps irresolvable,
conflict. I was travelling with a Mongolian. When we went into backstreet
restaurants in Kashgar, my companion had to refer to this non-Han —
and thus fellow "ethnic-minority" — origin almost the moment we walked
in, in order for us to get served. One evening, a local cadre took me
aside, at a small party organised by a friend. "Every day, all we do is
read the same old lies in the official Chinese press," he complained "how
do you think it feels like, going around all your life just to be identified

as a 'minority'? Is that all I am? A 'minority'? In most of the cities in this area, I am in the majority. Who the hell has the right to say I am a 'minority'?"

I remember one celebrated local academic I heard about in Urumqi. He had been working on a history of the Uyghur people for decades. A few months before his *magnum opus* was due to be published, some proof copies had been taken from his publishers, and the whole project stopped. Even a straight narrative history was problematic.[1] There was oblique talk of a well-organised resistance group abroad, based in Kazakhstan, with sympathisers as far away as Germany and the US. But even the most optimistic Uyghur nationalists admitted that their movement lacked two fundamental things: clear leadership and international sympathy. A decade and a half on, things have not improved.

In the interim, there have been moments of turmoil and violence. There were riots in Yili and other Xinjiang cities in the mid-1990s which resulted in many deaths and a surge of police and security personnel into the area. Even more shocking for the central authorities, an Uyghur group carried out a bomb attack on a Beijing bus in May 1997 which killed two people and injured 100. But it was the aftermath of the 11 September 2001 terrorist attacks that was to prove most significant, for it reshaped the US understanding of Xinjiang, and its dialogue about this key strategic area with the Chinese government. Two Uyghur groups were put on the US state department's internationally accepted terror list and 17 Uyghurs detained in Afghanistan and transferred to the prison camp at Guantánamo. In return, the Chinese became biddable allies in the wars in the Middle East. It was a good deal for the Beijing government, keen to press more severely on restive elements in a region richly endowed with natural resources, and central to China's access to even greater goods in central Asia.

Xinjiang, however, always posed immense problems to the central government, far harder perhaps than even than those of Tibet. The brief, bitter experience of independence in the 1940s was brutally crushed after Stalin's agreement with Beijing that Xinjiang was best subsumed within

---

[1] The history of Xinjiang from ancient to modern times is dealt with even handedly by James A Millward, *Eurasian Crossroads: A History of Xinjiang*, C Hurst, London, 2007.

the new People's Republic of China, which had historic claims on the area dating from the 18th century. Han migration into the region, planned and unplanned, continued into the 1950s and 1960s; it was led initially by a wave of settlers from the coastal cities seeking a new life and responding to the call to rebuild the motherland, then continued by youths "sent down" during the Cultural Revolution in the 1960s and 1970s (many of whom were simply left behind when this period ended).

Xinjiang was the place where China's first nuclear bomb was tested. It was the place, in the worst period of the Cultural Revolution, where mosques were shut down, and, in some cases, destroyed; where *imams* were forced to eat pork as a sign of their fidelity to Maoism, not Islam. Some of the Han settlers assimilated. They learned the local language, and tried to fit in. But by the 1980s and 1990s, a further wave of migration meant the arrival of many new settlers far too numerous to be easily assimilated. Many appeared to have been displaced by the Three Gorges Dam project in south-western China; at the time I was in Urumqi in 1995, rumours were circulating of trains bringing in thousands of such people.

By 2009, Xinjiang looks like a place with a delicate ecosystem placed under impossible pressure. Just as much of its natural resources now are being exhaustively exploited, so the area has an impossible mixture of Han, Uyghur and other minorities, including a large number of Mongolians in the central region. It is now a territory with a population almost evenly divided between settlers and local groups that are themselves ethnically, religiously and culturally different. Tensions have evidently been building. What happened on 5–6 July 2009 could be a mere precursor to much, much worse.

Xinjiang's tragedy is that it is a place where the central leadership cannot, for the sake of its own legitimacy, compromise. But in order to solve the problems of this area, it would have to change the whole pattern of its thinking about the treatment of border areas inhabited by minorities. The demand, then, must be of a new kind of boldness and vision from a group of leaders who have hitherto shown not the slightest clue that they possess these qualities. The initial repression and the blaming of "outside" forces for the unrest are all too predictable. But what to do about the long-term problem of Xinjiang would tax the imaginations and will of even the most brilliant and best-placed leaders.

In spring 2008, someone I was talking to about the Tibet riots commented that Xinjiang posed far harder choices. I didn't agree at the time, but my interlocutor was right. The unity of the People's Republic of China is most challenged not in the high oxygen-starved plateaus of Tibet but in the vast, half-empty plains and deserts of Xinjiang. And, most unfortunately for the people of Xinjiang — on both, on all, sides — this is a battle that the Communist Party and its current leaders feel they cannot afford to lose.

Gao Zhisheng and China's Question

3 February 2010

I have never met the Chinese lawyer and writer Gao Zhisheng, though on the recommendation of a friend I read his autobiography *A China More Just*[2] when it was published in Chinese in 2007. His tale of being harassed by security officers and police while defending the rights of those who were being prosecuted for following the quasi-religious Falun Gong movement (outlawed in China in the late 1990s) gives a fine view of the darker side of life for many citizens of the modern People's Republic of China.

It was clearly Gao's intention to raise the sights of his readers and enable them to connect his own story to that of the country as a whole. As he said on the publication of his book, "It is my hope that those who read my essays and those who know the hardship that surrounds my family and me will not view it as hardship that merely a few individuals are facing. It is actually a window through which one can see the lasting pain of a nation."

The willingness of Gao (himself a Christian) to take on highly contentious legal cases was always a risk. In December 2006, he was given a three-year jail sentence for "inciting subversion"; this was suspended, though he remained under tight surveillance. In 2007, he wrote an eloquent denunciation of the official treatment of some of China's "bad elements" for the US congress. His reward was to be detained by security personnel in September 2007 and placed for weeks in the same kind of hell as those he had been defending. He wrote a searing account of his experience; it

---

[2]Gao Zhisheng, *A China More Just*, Broad Press USA, New York, 2007.

describes one thug urinating on him, another sticking toothpicks in his testicles, and a third telling him "this is personal, you bastard" and that he won't get out alive from the "treatment centre".

Some of those who met Gao Zhisheng after his release say that he emerged from this experience half-dead, psychologically damaged, even a broken man. But his ordeal deepened: in February 2009 he was abducted in Shanxi province in central China, reportedly while seeking to leave China (he had already helped his wife and daughter to get to Thailand, whence they reached the US in March 2009). After his disappearance, Gao became a non-person: no trial was held, no charges brought, no official statement was made, nothing more was heard of him. Gao Zhisheng vanished.[3]

In September 2009, Gao's brother approached the public security bureau and asked whether there was any news of his whereabouts. He received the baffling reply that Gao had "gone missing while in detention"; perhaps an indirect admission that in fact he was dead, or in such a poor physical state after yet more ill-treatment that it was no longer possible to show him to the world. In January 2010, a journalist's inquiry for more information solicited another display of masterful ambiguity from a Chinese foreign ministry spokesperson, who declared that "Gao is where he should be".

It must be said that such blank refusal by the Chinese authorities to say anything at all about the fate of dissidents or other figures of concern is most unusual. Even the most hardline Chinese officials would see such stonewalling as counterproductive, and offer a statement (however terse) with at least some details about the individual's whereabouts, sentence and/or health. The silence that surrounds Gao Zhisheng feels like a live burial.[4]

The behaviour of a Chinese government that allows its agents to seize its opponents on the streets in broad daylight, then silences and buries them, seems to confirm the claims of its fiercest critics, namely, that this government is little short of a mafia on a massive scale. Is this really the way that the China's rulers want to be seen, by the world and their own people?

---

[3]Andrew Jacobs, "China's Defiance Stirs Fears for Missing Dissident", *New York Times*, 2 February 2010.
[4]Clifford Coonan, "Did the Chinese security forces kill Gao Zhisheng?", *Independent*, 16 January 2010.

Gao Zhisheng's true fate remains to be established.[5] But his principled stance and refusal to be crushed has at least shone some light into one of the darkest areas of the Chinese state's operation, its system of "black jails"—semi-legal, underground detention-centres where vexatious petitioners who have travelled to Beijing from the provinces are incarcerated by contractors and "dealt with". The roughness of the treatment meted out in these institutions is designed to intimidate citizens in search of voice and redress, and highlight the risks of such insolence to anyone (such as their neighbours at home) with similar ideas.

It is becoming harder for the state to protect this network of "black jails" from scrutiny. The rape of a female petitioner in one of these centres in 2009 caused outrage, with the guilty guard caught and prosecuted. A Human Rights Watch report[6] contains many case studies and details of the system's operation, and the fact that this report has been openly discussed in some parts of the mainland Chinese media reflects awareness in the country of problems in the conduct of the security service and police.

There is a strong argument that the Chinese leadership's rhetoric about a "harmonious society" is a masquerade which ill conceals the fact that this is a society in ferment, indeed that China is in the midst of an era of contention that began in the late 1990s. The central provinces illustrate this all too clearly. Places like Henan and Hunan are vast battlegrounds between business elites and state officials, with civil society groups and grassroots organisations also seeking to wield influence among the powerful. The courts are clogged up with various kinds of suits where groups try to gain advantage over another. There are frequent social protests, with some areas in the countryside unable to hold village elections because they disintegrate into mass pitched battles between different factions, clans or families.

A Pew Research survey conducted in 2008 found that 86% of Chinese were satisfied with the way things are going in their country. More detailed questions based on ground-level sentiment tend to give different results.

---

[5]Gao was interviewed by journalists in March 2010 and sentenced to three years in prison in 2011. As of December 2013 he was reportedly in Xinjiang.

[6]Human Rights Watch, *An Alleyway in Hell: China's Abusive 'Black Jails'*, November 2009. Available online at: http://www.hrw.org/reports/2009/11/12/alleyway-hell-o. Accessed 22 August 2013.

A survey of public trust by *Xiaokang* magazine in 2009 revealed that local government officials were less trusted than prostitutes. True, central government officials were rated slightly higher, but trust in them had declined in successive years.[7]

The handling of Gao Zhisheng (like that of Liu Xiaobo) is all the more remarkable in light of China's emerging status in the world — something vividly on display at the World Economic Forum in Davos. China is now a global power, with an economy that is integral to the rest of the world's; it is the world's largest exporter, and holds USD2.4 trillion of foreign-currency reserves; it has the world's largest-standing army, and wields diplomatic clout from Latin America to Africa, and from the Middle East to central Asia; and it has a big responsibility to help make a difference on key international issues.

Yet with all its might, China also sees individuals such as Gao Zhisheng as a threat. The evidence suggests that the central government has given at least passive consent to a particularly zealous, brutal and "deniably" renegade arm of the security services to arrest Gao and do whatever they wish with him. The question that arises is: are Politburo members — now used to massive security protection and a five-star welcome in almost every country in the world — happy to see Chinese citizens casually deprived of rights and even life? Or are they unable to reign in their own security services and hold them to account? To find the correct answer is also to understand where China is going.

China and Liu Xiaobo: The Weakness of Strength

11 October 2010

The Chinese writer and prominent legal activist Liu Xiaobo was subject to the travesty of a brief court process on 23 December 2009 and given a brutal sentence of 11 years two days later. The decision ended a year of uncertainty surrounding the dissident who, in December 2008, had publicised the call for civic rights and freedoms known as Charter 08; his trial came six months after he was placed under "house arrest" (at a detention centre which in

---

[7]Wu Zhong, "Sex and China's credibility gap", *Asia Times*, 12 August 2009.

fact was not his normal place of residence), itself six months after he was arrested and placed formally under investigation over his role in the charter.

The speed of China's physical transformation — ever-taller buildings, ultra-modern cities, high-speed trains, grand civic buildings — can conceal from view the deep immobility in other areas. In 1994, when I was based in the northern city of Hohhot in Inner Mongolia, it was only through acquiring a copy of the *Guardian*'s weekly overseas edition that I learned of the fate of the most renowned dissident of that era, Wei Jingsheng. He had already spent 14 years inside for his pioneering role in the "democracy wall" movement of 1978–1979, when he famously called for the government to embark on a "fifth modernisation" to match the four it had committed itself to: namely, democracy.

Soon after being released in 1993, Wei's refusal to remain quiet and the irritation of the paramount leader Deng Xiaoping led him to be sent back for trial. In a hasty one-day hearing in Beijing on a cold and subdued January day, he was condemned to another 14 years. I remember looking at the newspaper photo of the police deployed in the areas around the courtroom, keeping foreign reporters as far away as possible. Wei had not been properly seen or heard from for a long time. I felt greatly impressed by the courage he must have had to stand against this sort of isolating onslaught.

Wei was released in 1997, after constant pressure on Beijing from the US, the EU and others. Years later, I met him in London where he was giving a speech at an Amnesty International event. His sprightly, sharp humour was undiminished by almost two decades in prison. I told him of an incident in December 1999 when, as a foreign official in London, I had been given a list of high-level Chinese leaders to whom Christmas cards should be sent on behalf of Britain's then foreign secretary, the late Robin Cook. I just managed to prevent the despatch of seasonal greetings to Deng Xiaoping, who had died two years previously. Wei Jingsheng was both greatly amused and seized on the point that bureaucratic incompetence was truly universal among states.

Liu Xiaobo will need the same sort of resilience as Wei Jingsheng's to survive, and perhaps he too will one day be let free to live in the West. But whatever the future holds in his case, there is about China's treatment of its most prominent "internal" dissident a vengeful harshness that sends a bleak signal. Liu's greatest violation in the government's eyes was to draft the Charter 08 document that was to be signed by hundreds of Chinese writers and intellectuals. In itself, the charter is little more than a lucid call for greater transparency and openness, but at least a couple of its sentences have evidently irritated the most powerful leaders in China very deeply. Their treatment of Liu is a stark message to its supporters inside and outside China: if you mess with us here, we will annihilate you, so get on and make money like everyone else, while leaving matters of rights, law and democracy well alone.

There is, independently of Liu's statements or the way he has presented them, a puzzling element about this attitude. Why do the peaceful actions of one individual, who is barely known in the West, provoke this extreme fury? The Chinese government, after all, has become used to acting with brusque confidence in the international arena; its performance at the Copenhagen climate change summit in December 2009 (which came soon after it had secured an abject statement from Denmark from its leaders for meeting the Dalai Lama in May), is but one example. It seems extraordinary that a sovereign nation of 1.4 billion people, the world's largest exporter with over USD2 trillion in currency reserves, can demean itself by acting in this way.

China's inability to ignore Liu Xiaobo, or merely to rebut his statements and leave it at that, leaves it looking weaker than before. For in its response to such cases, the mighty Chinese government begins to look a much frailer thing, and less a dynamic, thrusting superpower-in-waiting than a fragile, insecure state. The day that China feels no need to force its immense hands over the mouth of a single individual's mouth for fear of him having the strength to speak out will be the day that it really will have risen, and be ready to shake the world. The treatment of Liu Xiaobo argues against that happening any time soon.

Liu Xiaobo and China's Future

12 October 2010

The awarding of the Nobel Prize for Peace to the imprisoned Chinese rights activist Liu Xiaobo on 7 October 2010 is a moment rich in significance for all involved.[8] For the dissident movement in China, it gives its cause

---

[8]Liu Xiaobo was joined by author Mo Yan as a Nobel Laureate when the latter was award the literature prize in 2012.

a lease of life. For those Western governments that have been saying less and less about specific human rights cases in China, it offers an occasion to reflect on the justness of this course. For the Chinese government, most predictably of all, it presents the chance for another angry burst of rhetoric (and an accompanying clampdown on other critical voices).

Yet Beijing's quaint denunciation of the award as politically motivated is also in its way confirmation of the reality that the prize is indeed political to its core. After all, its recipients have included (apart from genuinely worthy figures) a serving US President, former terrorists and (perhaps most galling of all) Henry Kissinger. But that is precisely what makes Liu Xiaobo a particularly appropriate winner.

Many have commented in the days since the award that Liu Xiaobo is far from well known in China, and that his victory will never be significant there. This is irrelevant as well as untrue. The key "targets" of his prize are the members of the Central Committee of the Chinese Communist Party, and especially those who sit on its Politburo. This elite *certainly* knows who Liu is, largely because its authority would have been required to send him to jail for 11 years in December 2009.

Now, China's top leaders are forced to respond to this latest piece of Western effrontery. The details of their discussions may not be known for a long time, if ever. But when they next convene around the tables of the Zhongnanhai (the central government compound in Beijing) to review their policy of harmonious social development and peaceful Confucian rise, there is bound to be embarrassment that a prize once deeply coveted by the Chinese government, is going to a Chinese national in prison in China. It is even more painful than the giving of the Nobel Prize in Literature a decade earlier to Gao Xingjian, which happened at a time he was exiled in France.

This is not the way the ultra-controlling Chinese political elite wants things to happen. So when the bad news came, it and the source of power it commands (including the media) was unable to react in an astute and (perhaps, from its perspective) effective way; that is, by adopting an attitude of lofty disdain towards this insignificant piece of frippery by an ignorant West. Instead it raised the decibels for the entire world to hear. The elite, by showing how much it cared about Liu Xiaobo's award, thus granted the Nobel committee an even greater success. The latter, by exposing in raw form one of the rare current vulnerabilities of some of the most arrogantly powerful people on the planet, can be well pleased with its work here.

Again, this is indeed a political rather than a cultural issue. The Nobel Peace Prize *should* aim to irritate repressive and unpleasant elites, whether in Africa, Asia, the Americas or Europe. The Chinese say they will set up their own prize to recognise international efforts, perhaps naming it after Zhou Enlai. They could then borrow from Europe and award it to individuals who might be irritating to power groups in the West. This would be very welcome.

More broadly, a definite outcome of Liu Xiaobo's Peace Prize is that it might mean fewer high-minded lectures from the Chinese Communist Party's "learning orientated leadership" about the Party's moral as well as economic prowess. The experience of seeing powerful and ruthless politicians adopt the dress and tone of gentleman scholars or solicitous uncles is already hard enough to stomach; a shift from this humbug and evasion towards realism would be beneficial all round.

China's leaders have in their stewardship of the economy over the last three decades demonstrated that they are competent in this area, perhaps even to a level of greatness that no one can deny and which deserves to be celebrated. But the extra dimension so often attributed to them — of being significant figures in cultural, intellectual and even spiritual terms — is a ludicrous fantasy. In this sense, this Nobel Peace Prize performs a function equivalent to that of the best political satire in the West, by showing China's communist elite in its true perspective.

Hu Jintao and his colleagues will continue to swim in a sea of serene self-righteousness in the image they seek to present to the world. But amongst the endless self-referential harmony of contemporary official China, this rude interjection will antagonise and unsettle the very people most in need of it.

Perhaps, then, at their next Zhongnanhai meeting the members of the Politburo can begin to reflect on the comic absurdity that they oversee the world's second-largest economy, the world's largest holder of foreign reserves, the world's largest exporter, and yet rule a country whose sole internationally recognised laureate is incarcerated for exercising his freedom of speech. And, with all this in mind, to take their own adage seriously: "seek truth from facts".

Hada, Liu Xiaobo and China's Fear

With Natalia Lisenkova

8 December 2010

The award of the Nobel Peace Prize to Liu Xiaobo reflects the determination of at least part of the international community to maintain a focus on human rights in China and those who seek to uphold them. By the same token, the immense energy that the government of the People's Republic of China is putting into the effort to dissuade representatives from foreign governments attending the award ceremony in Oslo on 10 December 2010 is a reminder of the lengths to which this highly authoritarian regime will go to project its own version of reality.

When the Communist Party elite sees what it defines as its core interests threatened, it is ready to deploy in the international arena methods that give foreigners but a taste of what it imposes on China's own outspoken citizens.

Liu Xiaobo is now the most prominent of the latter: China's best-known dissident still in jail in the People's Republic of China. His case — a citizen with a record of rights activism from the era of protest at Tiananmen, who was sentenced to 11 years of imprisonment on 25 December 2009 — raises many questions about what the regime in Beijing thinks about itself, and about its response to any challenge to its monopoly on power. Yet, in the absence of any answers from leading representatives of this regime (no Politburo member has as yet deigned to voice an opinion on Liu's treatment), the most striking thing about its action here is that it is shot through with fear.

The handling of Liu Xiaobo — his arrest, his jailing, the silencing of his wife and the reaction to his Nobel Prize — reveals anything but leaders confident and secure in their position. The very publicity given to Liu's predicament, which the Nobel Prize further fuels, at least affords him some level of protection. But there are many individuals serving jail terms in China now about whom far less is known yet who deserve an equivalent measure of attention.

One of these is a man called Hada, a native of Inner Mongolia who in 1995 was sentenced to 15 years of imprisonment. Hada, along with his wife Xinna, was the proprietor of a small bookshop in the centre of the provincial capital, Hohhot. Those who visited it would have seen nothing more than a place to buy Mongolian music, Mongolian-language tapes for prospective learners, and some small imported goods from across the border in the Mongolian People's Republic. The court deposition, however, alleged that it was the centre of an organisation agitating for a pan-Mongolian state, and secession from the People's Republic of China. There may indeed have been some truth in this.

Hada himself was also said to be a separatist who sought Inner Mongolia's independence, and was agitating for support amongst the 10% of the region's population who are (like Hada and Xinna) ethnically Mongolian. They had links, it was claimed, to groups in the US and Germany. Over 230 other suspects were seized in summer 1995, some of them connected to protests in the early 1980s. Many of these were also given heavy sentences.

Hada, the claimed ringleader, was given special attention after his sentencing. He was first incarcerated in Baotou, a large industrial city to the west of Hohhot; then transferred to Chifeng, a city to the north of the autonomous region. He was treated very harshly — as his wife reported in regular bulletins over the years — with beatings at the hands of other prisoners, mounting health problems and disturbing reports of neglect verging on a form of torture.

Hada has served a full sentence, and is finally due for release on 10 December 2010. But his future is far from assured, for in China's legal environment, the boundaries of a jail can stretch beyond its physical walls. Indeed, the Southern Mongolian Human Rights Information Centre reports that Hada's wife and son were detained on 4–5 December in Hohhot, amid reports that Xinna may be charged in connection with the running of the family's bookshop.

The case of Chen Guangcheng, a blind activist freed in September 2010, is further illustration of this. Since returning to his home in Shandong province, Chen has had no contact with the outside world. His home is surrounded by intrusive security, with lights kept on 24 hours a day, no visitors allowed in and no telephone or internet contact with the outside world. Liu Xiaobo's wife has been treated to similarly oppressive management. She has been detained, wholly against China's own laws, in her home. She has broken no laws nor been convicted of any crime, yet she might just as well be in prison. It can be presumed that this overbearing surveillance awaits Hada too. The arrest of his family is but the latest ominous sign that his freedom of movement will be severely restricted and his home become the kind of prison that those of Chen Guangcheng and Liu Xiaobo have.

The leaders of the Chinese Communist Party are some of the most powerful people in the world. They command an economy that is now the second largest after that of the US. They possess nuclear weapons, and formidable armed forces. They wield immense authority both in Asia and, increasingly, across the globe. But they also feel it worth their while to use every single method at their disposal, no matter how crude or demeaning, to crush opponents who — even in the best of times — are both weak and barely noticed among the wider society.

The sheer pettiness that characterises the repression they have authorised on Liu, Hada and many others is unseemly. But it is also instructive. For the mighty Beijing leadership seems actually to fear — that word again — that one or more of the weak opponents it has consistently tried to destroy will mount a real challenge to its authority; and that acting the way it does postpones such a dreadful outcome. The self-defeating aspect of the elite's course is that it only brings closer that nightmarish prospect.

The People's Republic of China is one of the most important powers in the world. Its continued emergence poses an unavoidable test not just of political capacity but of moral authority and legitimacy. To pass it, the current leadership needs to begin to temper its strength with justice and mercy. The experience of Hada, Chen Guangcheng and Liu Xiaobo — and many others — shows how far there is to go.

Inner Mongolia: China's Turbulent Secret

21 June 2011

Inner Mongolia is the least understood of China's major border autonomous zones. It is also, arguably, the most integrated. Tibetans make up 95% of the population of Tibet, Uyghurs compose about 50% of Xinjiang's, but Mongolians account for only 10% to 20% in their own so-called autonomous region. Moreover, the fact that the area is closer to Beijing, is more densely populated, and has been settled for a longer time by largely Han migrants, means that it might be expected to be the most stable.

These factors make the explosion of protests after the death of a Mongolian herdsman in a road accident in May 2011 all the more worrying for the authorities. The herdsman was run over by a truck driven by a Han in a northern area which has seen big exploitation of its mining resources. Mongolian local people were furious at what they saw as the murder of an innocent man.

The attitude of the culprits was interpreted as disdainful, and the slow response of the local government reinforced the anger. By the third week in May, there were student demonstrations in the provincial capital of Hohhot; the Party boss there, Hu Chunhua, was obliged to meet with some of the students and reassure them that everything would be done to bring the criminals to justice. But a single incident, as so often in China, embodies a far larger story.

Inner Mongolia's recent history is unhappy, and its people have perhaps more reason to be resentful than those of any other of the main border regions. They suffered horrific purges in the Cultural Revolution from 1966, when a whole generation of ethnically Mongolian officials, intellectuals and others were accused of harbouring ambitions to create a pan-Mongolian state (that is, unifying with the Mongolian People's Republic across the border).

Even official statistics, released in the early 1980s during a partial "rectification", acknowledge that 22,000 were killed in this period. But tellingly, the man in charge of the area in its most violent phase, Teng Haiqing, died in Beijing in 1996 without ever having been brought to justice.

The rooted frustrations among Mongolians over the lack of freedom and opportunity for their ethnic group and the more precise sense of betrayal and anger following the Cultural Revolution extended into the 1980s. There were student demonstrations in 1984, 1987 and 1989. In the mid-1990s, a major state clampdown led to the arrest of over 250 alleged "activists"; one of them, the bookshop owner Hada, was released only in 2010 (although he has since disappeared).

Meanwhile, the economic background has been transformed since 2000, as rapid creation of wealth has engendered new social and political dynamics in Inner Mongolia. Until the mid-1990s, the region was relatively backward and poor, with only very limited foreign investment.

But in 2000, as China's energy needs were exploding, the region's plentiful coal and other minerals suddenly became of great interest to the central government. In 2010, a six-day traffic jam on the road from Inner Mongolia into Beijing, almost all the trucks filled with coal, became a major news story. The energy of the capital, and of elsewhere in China, is fired by Inner Mongolia's resources, and this has made some people there very rich.

A visitor to Hohhot in 1996 and again in 2011 would doubt they were in the same place. The Hohhot of only 15 years ago still had old buildings, only a couple of towers above ten storeys and a sleepy airport; today, the city is enjoying (at 36%) the fourth-fastest growth-rate on the planet, and 200 new cars are registered every day for use on its roads. These are the boom years.

But the boom has brought great problems: environmental degradation (including terrible desertification), a critical lack of water accentuated by population growth and a series of very hot summers and freezing winters. The social and economic impact has also been very uneven. Many Mongolians are wholly excluded from the new riches, and are in thrall to a local business elite who can behave with ruthless brutality. Inner Mongolia is one of the most corrupt provinces in which to do business, and one where the security agents have a particularly vicious reputation. For the losers of the economic reforms, and those who happen to be ethnically Mongolian, the good times for others reinforce how much and how rapidly outsiders have changed their society.

The central and local government have responded to the latest protests in standard fashion, as in Tibet (2008) and Xinjiang (2009) with a harsh crackdown. So far, it has worked. No doubt, a little more money will be spent on social projects in the area to placate people. But both problem and solution in Inner Mongolia reinforce the sense that the Chinese Communist Party still maintains its ultimate commitment to economic growth, money and material outcomes over everything else, and that its solution to almost everything is to put money into it.

There is no sense that the government is thinking harder about its highly limited view of modernity, and about the alternative modernities that other cultures within the state's own borders might be able to offer. Beijing noisily proclaims its multicultural credentials, but a closer analysis shows that at heart the Chinese state maintains a crushing conformity wherein there is almost no space for those with different, alternative or contrary views.

The worry for the central leadership must be that along a ribbon of territory that divides China almost by half, big disturbances have occurred in the last three years. But there is almost no sign at the moment that the central government is rethinking its strategy. The economic crisis in the West since 2008 has proved China right, and no provincial troublemakers on its borders are going to change that.

Chapter Six

Following the Money: The Chinese Economy

Whatever the internal issues, it was universally accepted, inside and outside of modern China, that it was a place that was getting richer, and where the physical evidence of this wealth was increasing by the day. Cities like Shanghai and Beijing were daubed in the most outrageously modernist architecture commissioned by international practitioners to show their pride, their internationalism and their prowess. For Bentley, China became the second-largest market after the US and was catching up fast. Louis Vuitton had their largest branch in, of all places, the coal capital of Taiyuan, Shanxi province. Resource exploitation was creating wealth like never before, with newly enriched business people from the Chinese hinterland so cashed up they were able to buy apartments overseas, send their children to the best foreign schools and buy up most of the shopping centres they went to on their foreign holidays.

Chinese overseas investment was one of the new phenomenon, becoming more important from the early 2000s when the central government promoted a "going out" policy for its enterprises. But, despite the expectation over 2008 and 2009 of the Chinese investment funds and state-owned enterprises with their wealth coming out and buying up the brands and technology they needed across the world, the underlying tempo of this period was of great cautiousness. The paradox was that the world's second-largest economy from 2010 was such a minor outward investor. Perhaps part of this was due to the overreaction of so many commentators and "experts" as soon as China did decide to invest. Its battles through Huawei, partly state-owned, in the telecoms sector in the US, Australia and Europe became a cause célèbre *here.*

Most of the pieces here are from the fateful year 2009. Worries then that the global crisis would cause employment, exports and growth to plummet in China proved wrong. In fact, the government made the right call with a massive fiscal stimulus package, and growth kept into double figures from 2010. The deeper structural issues of low consumption, high capital investment, low services sector as part of GDP, and under-urbanisation (despite China moving from only 15% of its citizens living in cities in 1978 to just over 50% in 2010), things which the Vice Premier, and soon to be Premier, Li Keqiang referred to in his speeches from this time, were still figured as problems to be dealt with gradually in the future, rather than imminent causes of concern. The main thing for Hu and Wen was to make sure there was growth, growth, and then more growth. And this, despite the problems in the rest of the world, is what they did.

China Goes Global

2 August 2007

The epic process of China "going global" has been underway for over a decade, but the events of late July 2007 may well be its defining moment. The stake in Barclays bank purchased by the China Development Bank — one of Beijing's state-owned "policy banks" — is significant in itself, but it also represents a high-profile reversal of the dominant perception of China's international economic role.

Since China's entry to the World Trade Organization in 2001, foreign investors have salivated at the prospect of buying into a market with one of the highest savings rates on the planet (USD1.7 trillion sits in Chinese personal savings accounts). The Royal Bank of Scotland and the Bank of America (to name only two) have taken stakes worth billions of dollars in Chinese banks. But even a few months ago, the thought that China's own banking institutions might themselves undertake such bold action wasn't envisaged. The China Development Bank's acquisition of a minority share in Barclays was well judged — modest enough not to appear threatening, in tandem with a similar stake from Singapore's state investment arm, Temasek. At the same time, other observers see the move as the latest in a worrying trend whereby the Chinese state — in the form of seemingly innocuous enterprises — is creeping ever deeper into Western financial and economic institutions.

The economic story about China told abroad over the past decade and more has been about the phenomenal amount of foreign direct investment (FDI) flowing into the country. As of 2007, this stands at over USD700 billion in stockholdings. True, about 40% of that derives from the Hong Kong special administration region or the British Virgin Islands, and therefore is very likely to originate in China. Yet even with this qualification, China's ability to attract FDI has been impressive; since 1992 it has regularly featured as one of the top three FDI destinations.

But has this FDI really served its main purpose? For several years, the Chinese government has been signalling that all the money washing into China has not brought the technical partnerships and know-how that were originally expected. Of China's hi-tech exports in 2006, 88% were still made by foreign-investment enterprises, which operated largely by importing partly finished goods, using cheap labour to process them, and then re-exporting. China aspires to be a "knowledge economy", but in fundamental ways its current FDI regime has done little to help indigenous Chinese companies expand and develop. Chinese enterprises contain few global leaders, perform badly in innovation and score low on brand recognition. The Chinese government knows that somehow that model has to change.

A big part of this "somehow" is the government's encouragement of Chinese companies — which has been expressed since the mid-1990s — to "go out". This is unprecedented in Chinese terms, for China has never in history been an exporter of capital. Even a century ago, it was British and European countries that invested in China (mostly through Shanghai, and mostly in the energy and raw-materials sector). China did send out people and goods in past centuries, but it didn't plug into the global economy that then existed. That remained the case after the revolution in 1949 and throughout the early years of the People's Republic of China. Only in the 1980s, after the reform process inaugurated by Deng Xiaoping got underway and the Chinese economy opened up, did China start to invest in mining and raw materials (albeit in tiny amounts).

Today, things are moving at speed. China is the largest holder of foreign-currency reserve on the planet (it overtook Japan in early 2006; 70% of its USD1.2 trillion is in US dollars, USD 400 billion of it committed to US treasury bonds). The rest lies dormant, attracting low rates of interest and subject to currency fluctuations. In 2007, China has set up an investment fund, with an initial USD200 billion that it seeks to spend around the world. So far, it has committed USD60 billion abroad, most of it in Latin America and Asia, with increasing amounts in Africa. But gradually, Chinese companies are starting to have an impact, through mergers and acquisitions, in Europe and the US too. Chinese investment might still constitute less than 1% of the global stock, but that can only go one way — up!

Chinese overseas direct investment (ODI), however, faces the same problem as FDI into China, namely the fact that it is a highly politicised subject. FDI in China may have helped create a "non-state" sector, but — as many commentators have pointed out — the line where the state ends and the non-state begins in China can never quite be defined. Foreign investments in China have enjoyed high political status, but the very fact of dealing with the government and the Chinese Communist Party in China's uniquely politicised environment can complicate or undermine a "purely" business relationship

This applies to Chinese ODI also. The regulations may have changed to allow Chinese enterprises to search opportunities abroad without government sanction, but it remains the case that any investment of significance (and at the moment, most Chinese investments are significant) will need government support. Moreover, many of the corporations making the biggest impact overseas — like the China Development Bank, or the Chinese energy companies that are currently making waves in Africa and the Middle East — have direct connections to the government.

A number of cases illustrate this political problem. The China National Offshore Oil Company (CNOOC) effort to buy the US energy giant Unocal in 2005 was blocked because the US was unwilling to accept a bid with what looked like a large amount of Chinese government money in a key strategic industry. The purchase by the Chinese TV manufacturer TCL of Thomson in France has proved disastrous, at least in the European market where the management styles of the two companies seemed to come from different planets. Chinese "investment" in MG Rover in Britain and ThyssenKrupp in Germany involved — in public perception at least — a wholesale transfer of assets back to China with little contribution to the local economy to balance it.

The Chinese have appeared to be transmitting the message that the shift towards ODI is a strategy to compensate for the failure of FDI to provide them with the technical expertise they craved. This, and the fact that the one-party, non-democratic Chinese state lies behind it, has not been exactly reassuring to China's prospective commercial partners overseas.

But this is constantly changing as well as complicated story. Other investments, like Lenova into IBM's PC division in the US, and Huawei's into Europe, seem to be both working and adding value. The precedent for the Barclays venture — the stake taken by China in the US equity fund Blackstone — was regarded by informed analysts (notwithstanding public criticism in China itself) as strategic and smart. Friedrich Wu, an expert on Chinese ODI based in Singapore, argues that Chinese money invested in low-performing factories in Europe and the US can work to the advantage of both sides. Most significant, Chinese enterprises which go abroad tend to absorb some tough, hard lessons about the importance of corporate governance and company responsibility, which are fed back to China itself — thus assisting China in its great, long-term strategy of becoming a globally oriented economy.

The Chinese are learning quickly. In many ways, they have to. The World Bank has made clear that China's economic development since the mid-1980s has been faster, and vaster, than in any previous case, including of Japan after 1945. China's development in ODI is set to follow the same pattern. Now it has the responsibility of explaining to the outside world why its enterprises are not a threat, and why people outside China should be sanguine about the role of the Chinese state in them. That will need imagination as well as hard work. But there is no turning back. The Chinese buy-up is underway, and the world needs to be prepared.

China in 2009: A Year for Surprise

14 January 2009

The first weeks of 2009 find China consumed by the same anxiety as the rest of the world. No one in Beijing's top leadership wants a repeat of 2008's high-wire ride (the Beijing Olympics) and lows (the Tibet protests, the Sichuan earthquake, the contaminated milk-powder scandal). But the year of quiet development and consolidation that it might have hoped for is not in prospect, for China shares with other leading players, such as the US and the EU, the predicament of a global economy in deep crisis.

The realities of recent years are turned on their heads. China finds its exports shrivelling, and swathes of factories in the industrial Pearl River delta and elsewhere closed down. Perhaps 10 million workers, according to some estimates, have lost their jobs since mid-2008. There have been increasing reports of angry demonstration in the hinterland, with even normally reliable groups such as teachers in Xi'an, central China, striking in protest against poor wages and rising prices.

The averagely informed Chinese citizen is as baffled by everyone else by how much of a mess the US economy is in. The more conspiratorial see in the US predicament an international ruse designed to make them become a bit softer towards the world's final superpower. But the evidence of recession in the West, from financial indicators to the lengthening list of collapsed companies, show that this downturn is no clever game. Any hopes that China would somehow be insulated from the fallout have disappeared. A monument to this sobering reality is the swathe of vast five-star hotels thrown up in Beijing in the pre-Olympics months. Many now have a ghostly look as darkness falls, with a solitary lit window in a mass of darkened glass the only sign of habitation. The heat of high expectations has been succeeded by a cold shower.

China's leadership as well as its people are worried. Indeed, the country's cautious, pragmatic political elite is dominated by fear. The ruling party is effectively a state within a state, focused in the end on preserving its power, no matter what the cost. At least, this is the impression it would like to give others. A long-term resident of Beijing commented to me that President Hu Jintao and Premier Wen Jiabao see themselves as surrounded by potential threats, and that in response to anyone who dares to try to offer a competitive political challenge their trump-card is to deploy the power of the law, the army and the security services.

A case in point is the way that members of the Charter 08 group, led by veteran activist Liu Xiaobo, were rewarded with their declaration released on 10 December 2008 appealing to the authorities to allow more openness and political competition in China by being chucked into one of the "detention centres" in the suburbs of the capital. But Hu and Wen are careful to be seen as acting within the law, and in the strictest legal interpretation Liu and his colleagues are now no longer under arrest. They are just being subjected to "residential surveillance" and restricted in their movements and actions. It is an old trick, but for many years this tactic has worked, for it instils fear, isolation and, most wished-for of all, silence.

In their own terms, Wen and Hu are right. Mass unemployment, economic uncertainty, and rising threats to the party in power have never led to good things in the past. The smiling face that the world saw during the Olympics is at best wearing a weary grin at the moment. Tourists to Beijing and Shanghai may still perceive stability and calm, but those who look a bit closer see surprising levels of violence and discontent. For their part, the authorities are aware of the extent of unrest across China, from the demonstrations in the factory zones by recently laid-off workers demanding their wages from absconding Taiwanese owners to the upsurge of student anger directed against Japan in (of all places) the respected Fudan University in Shanghai.

When will these background murmurs start to become a shout, and then a roar? And if they do, how far will the Party be willing to go to keep a lid on things? Its past record is clear enough. If violence there must be, then so be it; the justifications and the cleaning-up can be dealt with later. It escapes no one's attention that 2009 is also the 50th anniversary of the Tibetan uprising of 1959 and the 20th anniversary of the Tiananmen protests of 1989.

So 2009 is going to be a tough year for China as well as for the rest of the world. The Chinese political elite seem keen to forge closer links with the US, and it will be looking to Barack Obama to help reinvigorate a relationship whose strains under George W. Bush have been hard to conceal. The 30th anniversary of the establishment of diplomatic relations between the two countries on 1 January 1979 — celebrated with a lavish two-day conference in Beijing on 12–13 January 2009 — might in principle be a propitious new beginning.

Yet the character of Obama's foreign policy is yet to be established. The early signs are that in any case the new President's main policy focus will be domestic: the need to clear up the mess his own country is in. Where China is concerned, the most intimate and yet fractious issue between the two countries is the same: trade. This has as much potential to cause dispute as cooperation, especially given the protectionist pressures likely to be exerted on the Obama administration. Moreover, it is unlikely that getting cosy with protocol-obsessed leaders in Beijing and helping them display their international credentials before their own people and the world will be one of Obama's priorities.

What might change the dynamic here? One thing that might is if the Chinese government suddenly took a positive, bold and unexpected action. It could, for instance, take the massive foreign reserves it has accumulated in the central bank, and make sensible, stabilising, strategic investments in the rest of the world.

It could also make a strong, proactive and defensible move to show international leadership, by demanding that international forums like the International Monetary Fund and the World Bank were fundamentally reformed to take greater note of the needs of developing countries, and be more representative of them. It could start genuinely to take a lead on the international efforts on climate change, or on energy security, or even on issues in Africa, where it has so many interests now. If it did any or all of these things, the world would sit up and take notice.

Something along these lines may well happen. This leadership may be bolder and braver than it can appear. The enigmatic smile of Hu Jintao might finally come to be seen as the stillness of wisdom, when China makes its move on the international front. While Western capitalism is sinking to its knees, the chance for China to show leadership looks like it has come. The critics are confident that they will be proved right and that China will remain fixated on its own problems, maintain a low profile, and do nothing on its own out front. But there is a chance that, sometime in 2009, China will act in a way that both surprises and shows the world that it has indeed become a major — and constructive — power.

If 2008 was a year when the prizes were awarded, 2009 will — one way or another — be a year of real endurance tests. But China will be competing for more than gold medal; it will be seeking the fair and proportionate position in the global economy and the world system that reflects how far the country has travelled. After all, 2009 sees yet another momentous event: the 60th anniversary of the foundation of the People's Republic of China in October. This is not a year to be timid.

The stakes could't be higher; nor could the rewards. The end of 2008 was marked by Western political leaders competing to claim that they had saved the world. The end of 2009 may yet become a moment for wide acknowledgment that in many ways, China just has.

China's Giant Struggle

5 February 2009

The leadership of the People's Republic of China faces economic and social challenges in 2009 that match anything comparable in the state's 60-year history. The visit by China's Premier Wen Jiabao to the World Economic Forum at Davos and to Britain, Germany and Spain signals that in many ways this leadership is both more confident than ever, yet acutely aware of how its power is constrained by its interdependence with others.

Wen's speech at Davos, in which he made the case that the US's economic-policy model bore great responsibility for the global economic crisis, reflects both realities; it was a mark both of how far China has come and how much its fate is bound up with its biggest trading partner. His positive appraisal of China's relationship with Britain (and his endorsement, including in a meeting with his counterpart Gordon Brown, of the ideas of Adam Smith's *The Theory of Moral Sentiments*) was likewise a striking display of diplomatic engagement.

The unflappable Wen proclaimed a "deep friendship between Chinese and British people" even in the face of an (Iraqi-style) protest in the form of a hurled shoe from an angry demonstrator. Those who recall the negotiations around the handover of Hong Kong to the People's Republic of China in 1997 might be astonished to hear such language, for at the time Britain was denounced each day in Chinese media for "hurting the feelings of all Chinese people". The British government's launch on 22 January 2009 of a strategic document outlining a new "framework for engagement" with China is evidence of a repositioning that seems to suit both sides. As if in confirmation, recent figures for Chinese investment to Europe show that Britain has overtaken Germany as the largest destination for Chinese money; proof that with the People's Republic of China, good money always follows the politics.

The domestic backdrop to the artful niceties and unexpected flurries of Wen Jiabao's foreign trip is awesome. A single figure tells a larger story: 20 million workers have lost their jobs as a result of the collapse of export markets for China's manufactured goods (moreover, the true figure is almost certainly millions higher). People of all backgrounds are affected: for example, university graduates who find that the decent positions they hoped for no longer exist. In part as a result, competition for scarce jobs in the civil service is more intense than ever.

Wen's repeated comment that China's greatest problems are internal seems vindicated, if not in the way that he would have wished. The result of the crisis is that the government's priority now is to maintain growth at a rate fast enough to create jobs and enough prosperity to keep discontent from boiling over. The lofty environmental and energy-efficiency goals contained in the "five-year-plan" (2006–2010) will need to be suspended as short-term calculation reigns.

The available reports of the multitude of current protests across China indicates that anger is being directed at factory owners (some of whom closed down and fled without paying wages) and local officials. China's central government (or, much more dangerously, the Communist Party) are not being specifically targeted. If that happens, the calculations will start to change.

The scholar Yasheng Huang argues that the 1989 protests were containable because they did not reach into the countryside.[1] Chinese economic policy in the two decades since has been largely urban-orientated, and in some ways created greater poverty in the country's rural areas.

Hu Jintao and Wen Jiabao's government has taken limited remedial action, lifting tax burdens on peasant farmers, allowing farmers to use their land as collateral for loans and talking about "people-centred socialism". Huang points out that the provision of education in rural China deteriorated in 1993–2003 to such an extent that an extra 30 million illiterate people appeared in Chinese government statistics in 2006. Chinese farmers are, relative to other social groups, poorer than they were two decades ago. Any large-scale discontent here is the central government's deepest fear.

That time has not yet come. But both Hu Jintao and Wen Jiabao are aware that with a difficult and tense domestic year in prospect, China needs to

---

[1]Yasheng Huang, *Capitalism with Chinese Characteristics, Entrepreneurship and the State*, Cambridge University Press, Cambridge, 2008.

avoid unnecessary political confrontation abroad or at home. The approach to the 20th anniversary of the Tiananmen Square protests in May–June 2009 will be especially nervous. Some on the more moderate wing of the Party expect a form of rehabilitation to be announced, for the event itself (still labelled a "counter-revolutionary" incident in official Chinese political discourse) and for the late Zhao Ziyang (ousted as Party Secretary because of his apparently emollient stance towards the students).

This is unlikely, though the symbolism of this anniversary (especially 4 June, the date of the crackdown) makes it particularly sensitive. It will be followed by the 60th anniversary of the founding of the People's Republic of China itself on 1 October 2009. The bombastic celebration that might be expected could sit ill alongside the economic and social effects of a continuing downturn.

There is enough reason here for the Chinese government and the Party, behind all their confident language, to feel vulnerable. China's dependence on its export markets and its linkage to the performance of the US economy, were evidently more fundamental than almost anyone realised. The policy response to recession has to take account of the deep interdependencies that have been forged. In this context, Hu's forthcoming talks with Barack Obama and other leaders, including at the G20 summit on 2 April 2009 in London, are even more urgent. China's year of build-up to the Beijing Olympics was — with the Tibet crisis, Sichuan earthquake and food scandals along the way — tough if (in the end) triumphant; this year of inescapable economic problems and potent anniversaries may make it look easy in retrospect. Hu Jintao in particular, the man with real power in the Party and therefore the state, will be tested as never before.

China Local, China Global

11 March 2009

In China's industrial zones today, there is a palpable feeling of the great wheels of this enormous, complex economy grinding down. The north-eastern city of Harbin is deep in state-owned-industry territory — part of the Heilongjiang region where the then Premier Zhu Rongji was in the 1990s willing to see millions laid off work in order to rationalise and streamline the state sector. After that painful period, what is happening now should be easier to digest. Much indeed looks normal. Tourists from Russia — the main source of foreign visitors and business people in Harbin — wander around the newly expanded ice festival in its stage set beside the Song River that runs grandly through the city centre. Yet the burgeoning black market generates rumours that the tourist zone Tiger Park is funding itself by running a sideline in tiger parts for Chinese medicine. Perhaps that is why these fierce animals scuttle away at the first sign of humans; they really do look terrified.

There are other reversals. It is hard for the college students I talked to who are facing unemployment as it is the first time in a generation this is happening. The government wants its debts repaid in 2009, on time — not (as in the past) kicked into a never-arriving future. The local colleges are being told to sell more land, or get more fee-paying overseas students (a familiar story to a visitor from Britain). The flash new shopping centres downtown look emptier than usual. A clothing factory in a nearby town is now heavily reliant on government procurement after private orders dried up.

In short, the credit crunch has arrived with a vengeance. The economic trends are feeding the power of local officials, and the undercurrent of complaints about corruption is becoming constant. But in the local institute for the study of Marxism–Leninism there is a feeling of vindication. Academics and researchers who survived through the (for them) tough years when the non-state sector was king and capitalism ruled in all but name now hint that they were right all along. The once-mighty system of Western capitalism is in deep trouble. It is a better time than it was to be a true-believing Chinese communist.

Those college students are competing for now prized, stable and secure government jobs. China's wealthiest man, the owner of the electrical-appliance manufacturer Goumei, has been arrested — another sign of entrepreneurship in retreat. The government leaders are talking the more familiar language of "people-centred socialism".

From the perspective of Harbin, the high-level global diplomacy in which this government is engaged seems far away. Yet the leadership in Beijing is acutely aware that its ability to manage the difficulties faced in the People's Republic of China's industrial heartlands is intimately connected with its relationships with overseas trading and financial partners, the US above all. This reality was on show when Hillary Clinton and her entourage descended on China on 20–22 February 2009, in her new role as US Secretary of State. The circumstances were notably different from those of her earlier high-profile diplomatic trip to Beijing in 1995, when — as the US "first lady" — she participated in the United Nation's fourth World Conference on Women.

This conference was for Beijing part of the long process of its international rehabilitation after the 1989 uprising, and a major morale boost after the shock of failing in 1993 in its bid to host the Olympics Games in 2000 (a decision that went in favour of Sydney by two votes). The event was surrounded by fractiousness: some groups were refused entry to China, others (largely representing minority groups within China) bundled away from the main conference venues. Hillary Clinton was relatively free to express forceful opinions, and in her way foreshadowed the public statement of her husband to his counterpart Jiang Zemin in October 1997 that — on the matter of the Tiananmen events and human rights in general — the Chinese leadership was "standing on the wrong side of history".

How times have changed! The then President Bill Clinton is now the kept man, while his wife has become the world's most powerful diplomat. Moreover, a US scarred by soaring unemployment in an economy in deep recession cannot afford combativeness towards a key global partner. The fact that Hillary Clinton's first overseas trip was to Asia rather than to the Middle East or even Europe can be taken to reflect Washington's reordered priorities at a time of exceptional stress.

The high stakes and high risks that now underlie the relationship were signalled by Clinton's apparently casual but evidently quite deliberate remark to journalists travelling with her by plane that the issues of human rights and Tibet must be put in a large context that embraces the economy and the environment too. If the momentous area of climate change is included — one where China's involvement is absolutely crucial — the rationale for an approach that favours political calculation over principled commitment is even clearer.

On their side, Chinese leaders are fully aware that their views and actions are taken more seriously in the world than ever. If Clinton's visit is one indication, Wen Jiabao's brief "trip of confidence" tour of five European states in January–February 2009 is another. (Even having a shoe thrown at him by a disgruntled researcher in Cambridge — a distinction shared with the world's previously most powerful man, ex-President George W. Bush — can be seen as a sort of tribute.) The next major indication will be the gathering of leaders of the world's largest economies in London on the occasion of the G20 summit on 2 April 2009.

There is cold logic at work in the current, delicate phase of elite diplomacy between Washington and Beijing. Both sides are anxious not to let issues such as Tibet or a discomfiting naval spat get in the way. Hu and Wen understand that no generation of Chinese leaders can afford to allow a return to the poverty and bloodshed of the past, but that they also need the rest of the world if they are to avoid this fate. The message of the good people of Harbin is that it will take more than a severe economic downturn to deflect them from their 30-year path of prosperity and development. The thread that connects the Chinese local and the Chinese global is more frayed than it was; but it has not yet broken.

Chapter Seven

After Hu Jintao

The leadership transition having been achieved, both at Party level in late 2012, and at government level during the National People's Congress in 2013, it was time to assess where the new leaders stood and what clues they might give to their likely future behaviour. Xi Jinping as the core leader in this group attracted particular attention because of his dense references, from the first day he became Party Secretary, to the need to fight corruption. This language sat uneasily with a wide awareness that, at almost every level, the Chinese Communist Party was corroded and affected by corruption, with even junior officials on the make. A few changes in terms of how cadres entertained themselves and how they travelled were presented as being profoundly significant. But there was widespread scepticism about how, in the end, when it was the source of its own discipline and rule observance, the Chinese Communist Party was able to combat larceny, greed and misuse of state funds by its own key cadres.

Perhaps this campaign was just an admission that the fundamental dynamics of Chinese society and the ways in which the rulers and the ruled related to each other were changing. Carnival China was a place where things were upside down — where officials lived in far greater fear from public attacks than perhaps in democracies simply because there were rising levels of anger and impatience and little effective legal or procedural routes to deal with this. One friend from Shanghai I spoke to whose parents were officials simply said that their mother had refused to pursue a complaint against a man who had struck her during a road rage incident because it would have attracted unwanted media and public attention and was best to simply let go. Another academic in 2013 complained that while officials in the West only had to fight against nosy journalists, in China they were up against a mobile phone-touting, film-taking, social media-savvy public

155

who were all too eager to place footage of officials stuffing their faces at expensive banquets or misbehaving online.

The leadership transition in some ways had been a distraction. The elite may have shuffled places and let in some new faces, let go a few older ones, but the most important story was the great transition in Chinese society itself, something that the Party and the government showed they were simply following in the wake of rather than truly directing. In 1978, the reforms of that era had unleased forces which had no clear-cut outcomes. By 2013, therefore, the most that could be said was that there was an uneasy reigning pact. The elite did what they needed to do in terms of setting political and broad economic objectives, and pranced around in their elite world, largely separate from the rest of society, mouthing their bizarre Party language, and the rest of society did whatever it pleased. A small minority strayed deliberately or by accident into spaces that irritated the Party — their treatment has been described in Chapter Five. For the rest, Carnival China was an exhausting, irreverent, chaotic, enthralling, tragi-comic place that more often than not defied easy categorisation. In these final pieces, therefore, I admit how, more often than not, in looking at this place called China and relating to many of the people in it, I was brought starkly up against my own values, my own sense of identity, and questions about who, in fact, I was that held these opinions about a place which had once figured, even in my own lifetime, as remote, mysterious and mostly unknown.

Chimes at Midnight: Corruption and the Future of the Communist Party

15 March 2013

Two decades ago a young official serving in one of the poorer regions of southern China mounted a local campaign against corruption. He spoke forcefully about the need for local officials to keep their hands out of business and be careful what they did. "If you want to get rich," he said, "then don't go into politics". Infrastructure and public project funds were being siphoned off at an alarming rate, and the start of the 1990s boom was also beginning to offer temptations to relatively lowly paid local bureaucrats which were, most of the time, hard to resist.

A decade later, after promotion, the same official sat at the centre of a whirlwind, as one of the largest embezzlement scandals to ever hit the country unfolded. A local businessman had created a network of officials and business people, in which billions of *yuan* of smuggled goods had come into the country, avoiding customs and tariffs. A scam this size would have been impossible to hide. The collusion of the local customs bureau was proved through a series of investigations. These reached the doors of the Politburo itself, with one member at that time implicated through his divorced wife in the whole vast network. Oddly, only one senior official in the province remained unscathed after this affair blew over.

That official got his reward. Promoted first to be Party head of Zhejiang, then, briefly, Shanghai, and then onto the Standing Committee of the Politburo, China's elite of elites club, Xi Jinping now has the full suite of titles to make him, in one fell swoop, the most immediately powerful figure in Chinese politics, at least on paper, since Hua Guofeng replaced Mao Zedong after his death in 1976. Where Jiang Zemin, and Hu Jintao had to wait over a period of one to two years for their collection of Presidency, Party Secretary and Chair of the Central Military Commission, Xi has gained these in less than six months.

What is more significant than his titles, however, is that he also seems to be showing a remarkable amount of political will. His speech on 15 November when he emerged finally as Party leader in Beijing was no rhetoric-strewn list of empty plaudits. Corruption and reaching out to the people were the two things he said which struck many observers at the time. He has often returned to these themes since, with powerful attacks on vested interest in January, and while at the National People's Congress in early March when he met a delegation from Shanghai. So he hasn't just got the job titles, he is actually seeming to act like he intends to do something with them.

All of this could be fodder for the masses. Leaders sonorously condemning corruption in China while doing nothing significant to combat it has become a mainstay of contemporary politics there. It is usually greeted with the same kind of resigned scepticism that leaders in the West receive from the public when they declare that they are acting on principle, not on Party interests. We know they have to say this, but we also don't believe them. Wen Jiabao, retired Premier, spoke about corruption being a threat to the very existence of the Party during his decade in office. But that didn't stop his immediate family, including his wife, son and mother, according to *The New York Times* in October 2012, making an immense amount of wealth.

But what is more intriguing about Xi, however, is that it seems, at least at this early stage, as though he is actually at the centre of a leadership which is willing to draw blood when it has to. A good example is government reorganisation. The received wisdom over the last decade or so has been that while there was every reason to create a super Ministry of Transport, the vested interest in the Ministry of Railways, which had become almost a fiefdom of powerful, rich officials and their families, was impossible to break. But at this year's National People's Congress, overnight this "unsolvable" conundrum was solved. The Ministry of Railways now no longer exists.

Campaigns to snare corrupt officials are nothing new. In the last five years, according to a report given by the Supreme People's Procuratorate in March 2013, 30 officials at ministerial level or above have been disciplined. It is too soon to see if this figure goes up much under Xi. The biggest fish to be caught so far is Li Chuncheng, former Vice Secretary of the Chinese Communist Party committee of Sichuan Province. The bottom line for Xi, however, is not to contribute to these statistics, but to carry his impressive bearing and pronouncements on corruption right against individuals of immense power in the system who are at the heart of the patronage and client network on which covert deals and immense money-spinning scams thrive. The big money is in the state-controlled areas of the economy, from energy to telecoms to construction, where the relationship between Party, government and business elites is cosiest, and the costs of political challenge highest. Nailing one of these will be worth thousands of smaller fish, simply because this carries the strongest message that rule of law applies to everyone.

Xi might be different to former leaders in this one respect. For him, if the stories about his previous attitudes to corruption while in Fujian given at the start of this piece hold any water, then his attitude to corruption shows that he profoundly believes that it infects the Party's wholesomeness and is an affront to a body that his family, and in particular his father, sacrificed so much for to bring to power. In that sense, for Xi this issue is personal, and that gives his language about it a missionary edge that the somewhat automatic pronouncements of former leaders lacked. He is backed up here by a sense that the boom years of Hu are coming to an end, and the luxury of tolerating the inefficiencies corruption brings has to be stopped. Now that Xi has found his theme, however, he'll need to show more of the hard-nosed political corralling and preparation that the Ministry of Transport move seemed to hint at. Even in a few months, however, we can start to see the outlines of a far more "political" and strategic figure than Hu Jintao ever was. And that is surely no bad thing.

On Networks and the New Leadership

15 May 2013

The father of modern Chinese sociology, London School of Economics-trained Fei Xiaotong, talked of relationships in China being based on a model of elasticity, with each individual at the centre of a world of connections and links. His most famous description of this, from a book *From the Soil*,[1] was written in 1947. Fast-forward 66 years, and despite the immense changes in China, in the area of these intimate and interpersonal links, in some ways little has changed.

This is particularly true if one is talking about the top levels of political power in contemporary China. In the confusion of 2012 and the build-up to the Party Congress which finally confirmed the leadership change in Beijing, even the most hardened, experienced analysts were caught second guessing. Would there be seven or nine or more on the Standing Committee of the Politburo? Would Hu Jintao stay on as head of the Military Commission? At the most desperate moments, some wondered whether there would there even be any leadership transition at all? Only around 15 November when the new faces finally emerged did the world know for certain. Thankfully, we can be spared this festival of speculation for another five years.

When I worked in the British Embassy in the early 2000s, I remember the fun of listening to those who used to advertise their deep links within the system. They would refer darkly to "informed sources" and to inside track

---

[1] Fei Xiaotong, *From the Soil*, UCLA Press, California, 1992.

connections who fed them reliable information. One of the most zealous practitioners of this modern form of fortune telling declared before 2007 that Zeng Qinghong would be appointed country President in the Congress that year, and that they had heard this from a totally impeccable source, deep within the government compound in Zhongnanhai. 2007 came and went — and so did Zeng Qinghong.

Robert Caro, in his justly celebrated biography of US President Lyndon B. Johnson[2] writes that one of the prime features of power is that it not only corrupts, but reveals. On the slippery slope up to the top you have to conceal, hoodwink, persuade and practice subterfuge. Once at the top, you can start relaxing a bit and do what you want. The odd thing in China, however, is that the concealment never really seems to stop. We have the final outcome of almost all aspects of the leadership transition in China — Party, military, most provincial, ministerial and government. Surely now we finally have the clues out in the open it should all start to make sense?

One of the things we might start to do, as we get to know this new leadership a bit better in China and begin to dismantle their skills of concealment, is to refresh and revise the frameworks through which we try to make sense of them. For a number of years talk of factions in China has been popular. Set interest groups have been defined, ranging from those with a common career link to Shanghai, to those who worked their way through the Communist Youth League, to those that are designated, as Xi Jinping often is, as princelings — Party aristocracy, with close relatives who were senior leaders in the earlier revolutionary generations.

Everything we learned from the leadership transition last year shows that we need to see things on a much more microscopic level now. The neat cohesion and coherence that faction-speak gives to Chinese politics doesn't work that well any more. The system is way more dynamic than that. People pick up, develop, discard, cultivate and recruit different individuals, or groups, in ways far more subtle than simply belonging to some neatly defined group. Within what we thought were factions, in fact, we can see multiple bands, interlinks and blurred boundaries. It is striking that in this

---

[2]Robert Caro, *The Years of Lyndon Johnson*, Volumes 1–4, Alfred A. Knopf, New York, 1982–2011.

new leadership, none of the figures fit neatly into any one silo. We have been compartmentalising too much.

Taking Fei Xiaotong's remarks from over six decades before, what we can see more clearly are individuals who are able to remain aloof from specific alignment to any particular group. The real players in modern Chinese politics are those that are somehow able to negotiate their way through different sets of vested political and economic or social interest, and emerge from it not being easily claimed by anyone, but able to operate mostly in their own space. Seen in this way, Xi Jingping is the most elastic and liquid of them all — someone who is politically aloof, doesn't fit easily into any one camp, be it provincial, military, tribal or political. Hu Jintao had a similar quality, as did Wen Jiabao.

Now that power in China has been marketised and valorised along with everything else, this skill at avoiding getting into the political debt of others too much, and spreading risk in the universe of networks around you is a pretty critical one. Patronage diversification is the new name of the game, and making sure that you extend your risk as far as you can, like someone trying to play the stock exchange, has become a key part of success. We've been able to get away for too long with the lazy shorthand of forcing the highly mobile, dynamic and shifting allegiances of modern Chinese politicians into over simple frameworks. Now we have to think way harder about how these networks, at the centre of a society that is itself profoundly networked, really work. That at least, now it is finally over, is the one great lesson I learned from events in China in the last year.

Time to Accept Difference

18 June 2013

Over 20 years of engagement with China means that most of the positions I once took up great certainty on have been eroded, or absolutely evaporated. When I lived in the Inner Mongolia region of China from 1994 for two years, I remember spending most days resisting any sense I was somewhere radically different from where I came from, and trying to pin down similarities. People talked of *guanxi* or connections in Chinese society then, of going through the "back door", of "losing face". But all of these things were comparable to phenomenon in my homeland. Beyond superficial differences, I thought, there wasn't such a massive chasm. I got to know people well who were as transfixed by the great tasks of getting on in life, falling in love, dealing with disappointment and setbacks, and achieving sporadic success and happiness as anywhere else I'd ever been. And when anyone started talking about the subtlety of Chinese communication, and the ways in which saying one thing often mean the precise opposite, I could fall back on experiences being born and brought up in the England, where this sort of practice is almost a national pastime.

Nowadays, things are way more complicated. Having supped at the healthy offerings of scholars like the late Edward Said's *Orientalism*[3] for many years I was strongly alert to anything that posited China, or any "Asian" culture for that matter as somehow encapsulating difference, or of being some sort of construct of "the other". In a speech in Shanghai in 2008, when asked how I had become interested in China, I boldly quoted the great historian Joseph Needham's statement that it was the final place where one would truly encounter a culture of profound and radical difference. A member of the audience took me to task, deploying the deadly term "orientalist". I took the rebuke, and grew warier still.

Of course, I still see, and seek, for common human behaviour when I am in China. Simon Ley's elegant line "we cannot learn any foreign values if we do not accept the risk of being transformed by what we learn"[4] is true — up to a point. But why call it a risk? This should be a joy, a happy thing, shouldn't it? The joy of engagement with China, therefore, is increasingly these moments when expectations are neatly tipped up, and suddenly the idea held so dearly before of sameness and easy common ground being everything is, well, made complicated and harder to stand by.

There are two recent examples of this. The first is the very different attitude to public official malfeasance. In the UK, four politicians were accused in late May and early June 2013 of behaving in ways they should not have. They have contested the charges. But the uniform media and public anger showed there was complete consensus here. Public officials

---

[3] Edward Said, *Orientalism*, Vintage Books, New York, 1979.
[4] Simon Leys, *The Halls of Uselessness: Selected Essays*, Black Inc, Melbourne, 2011.

just shouldn't do this. In China, the leadership under Xi Jinping since last November has, across the board, made strong statements about the evils of corruption. They have said far more explicit and forceful things than recent Western leaders have needed to say. And yet, almost at the same time, there is widespread knowledge of the overwhelming amounts of wealth that members of the families and networks around elite political figures have accrued. The stories of Wen Jiabao issued last year, and those about Xi Jinping's family by Bloomberg were two particularly powerful examples. Rumours swirl around almost every other major figure. How can one explain this odd dissonance? If leaders in China hate corruption so much, surely they need to reign in the people closest to them first? And if they can't do that, then surely using such loud language about corruption is only going to create public cynicism and disbelief, because they themselves are so impotent about affairs in their own back yard. Have we got this wrong? Are they saying something else when they use this language they seem to be deploying now? What is going on?

The other is Chinese views of their own role in the world. Liu Yunshan was head of propaganda in the Politburo before his surprise promotion last year. For a number of years he has produced essays in the Party theoretical magazine, *Seeking Truth*. These give insights into elite views on Chinese cultural influence and soft power. For Liu, it is simple. Any economic prowess that the Chinese enjoys these days must translate into influence. It not only must, but it should — it is a moral right. China has become rich, and therefore powerful, and therefore has the moral right to be regarded with more respect. This is what makes the series of negative news stories about China after 2009 and claims it was assertive and bullying very hard to take. Because it is rich and strong now, it should be admired, and the government formulations of the country's culture and traditions are the means to do this. End of argument.

Liu's tone in his speeches over the last few years capture well this sense from a key elite figure that the feeling of bewilderment across cultures is shared. "How on earth," he seems to be saying, "can people in Europe and America and elsewhere not see that we deserve, we merit, we must have their admiration." Hubris, arrogance — this is all of these things. But it captures well the sense of elite exceptionalism. Should we, should I, as someone engaged daily with China and trying to understand China, simply brush this aside with impatient disdain? How do I engage with this clear sign that someone who is now very important has this view of the world? And can I really do anything that would change the views of Liu, and of perhaps many like him working in the central propaganda structures? Does their belief that they are different in this way get changed by me being convinced that they have no right to think this?

We don't need an era of nostalgic orientalism, for sure. But we probably do need a more sophisticated vocabulary and framework to deal with understanding differences. China is a place of immense diversity. Getting a deeper idea of the sectors, strands and factions bound around common interests in China is an important task. Now we live in this wonderful moment when a country that I went to almost a quarter of a century ago when it was introspective — still a little closed on itself, still constrained — is opening out in ways I never expected I would see. Maybe we need to think much harder about some of the differences we see, and track down these moments of intellectual collision, when suddenly it's clear that despite all the common grounds and the shared understandings, we are able, and comfortable, in dealing with our differences. And trying to think a bit deeper about the ways that Chinese leaders talk about corruption and about their national image is an interesting place to start.

Index